e2
effectiveelders

FOREWORD

Since retiring from a located ministry in 2006 I have conducted monthly mentoring retreats for preachers. We spend three days talking about the thrills and challenges of leading the church. Surprisingly, the most lively and focused session is one that concerns elder-preacher relationships.

Since we have two silos of leadership in our structure there is often a tug-of-war to see who is really in charge. Sometimes there is so much bureaucracy and red tape that the church becomes dysfunctional. There's often a feeling of frustration with the ineffectiveness of meetings and occasionally a feeling of animosity exists between preachers and elders.

One preacher lamented, "I've been at my church for five years. We've grown from about 100 to 300 in attendance. We have four elders. One is gone so much he's disengaged and one is so passive that he doesn't ever want to disagree and ruffle feathers. The other two are very strong personalities and they have recently told me they want no more changes in methodology or programming because the older people are uneasy about all the changes already. I feel if we don't continue to make changes we won't reach the young people in our community. What should I do? Should I stay or leave?"

Preachers will say, "Our elders treat me like a hired hand" or "My elders never take the initiative. If I don't do it it won't get done." "In our church it's like the minister is supposed to be the visionary and the elders are supposed to stop him... or at least keep him from spending too much money." Few elder boards seem to function well.

Of course the dysfunction of the church isn't always the elder's fault. Sometimes the ineffectiveness can be traced to the preacher or a staff member who is lazy, unspiritual, unethical, controlling or lacking accountability or people skills. There is so much frustration in this area that new church planters are searching for ways to get around the system. Some don't have elders; they establish "Ministry teams" instead. In some places the paid staff make up the majority of the elders or the elders are the minister's hand-selected "yes men." Some have set up the Carville model of leadership in the church where the preacher is regarded as the CEO and the elders resemble a corporation's board of directors – they get a monthly report of what's going on.

Since the Bible specifies elders are to be the overseers of the church and since we are a people who respect The Book, we need to consider how to make the God-given system work more effectively I Timothy 3, Titus 1, and 1 Peter 5 are in the Bible for a purpose. The problem isn't with God's design, it's with our implementation of His plan.

That's why this book about the role of eldership is desperately needed and can be extremely helpful. James Estep, David Roadcup and Gary Johnson have the theological credentials and practical experience to shed some light on how God intended His church to be shepherded. Jesus Christ is still the only hope of the world, the church is still His body on the earth, elders are still the pastors of His flock and the times in which we live demand the best we can give. So study and implement the principles set forth in this book so the church can be as the Lord intended it to be -- a city that is set on a hill that cannot be hidden. "And when the Chief Shepherd appears, you will receive the crown of glory that will never fade away" (1 Pet 5:4).

Bob Russell
Louisville, Kentucky

Answer

Table of Contents

Introduction

Introduction to *Answer*

Healthy congregations require a healthy leadership. Without a healthy leadership, the odds of a congregation growing spiritually, let alone numerically, are greatly diminished. This is the principle concern of this series: Healthy leadership facilitates healthy congregational life. To ensure healthy congregations, we must give attention to the health of our leadership, the elders. This book endeavors to orient, inform, challenge, educate, and ultimately equip men to be leaders within the congregation, elders that genuinely lead and shepherd the flock of God.

Leadership that is Christian is based on God's *call* to service, one to which we must *Answer*. The man is qualified and equipped by a life representative of Christian *character*, maturity, *Reflect* His character. Further, an elder must possess *competencies*, abilities that serve him well as he leads and shepherds God's people; *Lead* His congregation. Finally, the *community*, both the congregation and its social context, provide the area for an elder to serve as a leader within the community of faith and a witness to the community around it as we *Enjoy* His people. All four are essential for Christian leadership to be effective, none of them are optional.

About the Series

This book is the first of a four volume designed to equip elders for effective leadership in the congregation by e2 ministries (www.e2elders.org). The four volumes (*Answer, Reflect, Lead, and Enjoy*) parallel the four basic components of Christian leadership previously explained. These books are not intended to be scholarly treatises of the eldership. Rather, they are designed as useful study guides that utilize practical and academic insights for elders. Each chapter is intentionally brief and concludes with reflective questions for your own personal use, or use as an eldership as a means of training and equipping one another for service.

Answer, Volume 1, addresses the divine call of the elder to serve as a leader within the congregation; a call that indeed deserves and requires an answer. Chapter 1 addresses the nature of the call placed on an elder's life as a leader within the congregation. Chapter 2 speaks of the spiritual conversion and transformation necessary in the life of an elder. The qualifications for eldership are surveyed in Chapter 3, while Chapter 4 provides models for the elder selection process. Chapter 5 introduces us to the idea of elder governance, what role and function an eldership plays in the life of a congregation. The final chapter discusses the value and importance of having elders accountable to other elders, spiritually and pastorally, through peer evaluations.

This book can be used in two ways. First, it can be used as an individual study, something that you as an individual elder within the congregation read for your own edification and education. You may be a new elder, or perhaps an experienced leader looking for additional perspective and insight. Regardless, the book integrates throughout the text a set of Reflection Questions designed to help you apply each chapter to your life as a Christian and an elder. A second way in which this book can be used is by your eldership. Each elder could read the book, use the Reflection Questions, but then make use of them to discuss the text together as an eldership. In either case, whether individual or group, we do hope the book is beneficial to your life and ministry.

About the Authors

This series is not the produce of one author. Rather, it is the fruit of three individual's labor, working in concert with one another, and bringing their diverse experience and perspective to the table for discussion. One of the authors is an academic (James Estep), another a church consultant (David Roadcup), and still another a churchman (Gary Johnson). While these three men have known one another separately for a long time, it was not until they were all three together  in Heiligenkreuz, Austria teaching students from eastern Europe and central Asia at *Haus Edelweiss* (TCMI) that the three men sat together for the first time and shared their concerns for the health of congregations and the health of its leadership. We are convinced that a healthy leadership builds a healthy congregation. From these conversations over coffee came the idea for this series, designed to strengthen the health of elders as the congregation's leaders. It further led to the founding of e2: effective elders ministries in September 2012 (www.e2elders.org).

While individuals were assigned their own chapters to write, the final form of each chapter was reviewed and reworked by all three authors sharing a common table, typically in Indianapolis, Indiana. Hence, the work is a tri-authored resource for the equipping of congregational leaders who serve as elders of the Church.

We are praying for you and your congregation, and if we may be of service, feel free to contact us at your convenience.

June 2012

James Estep, Jr.
Dean, School of
Undergraduate Studies.
Lincoln Christian
University
Lincoln, Illinois
Jim@e2elders.org

David Roadcup
Professor of Christian
Ministries
Cincinnati Christian
University
Cincinnati, Ohio
David@e2elders.org

Gary Johnson
Senior Minister
Indian Creek Christian
Church
Indianapolis, Indiana
Gary@e2elders.org

Chapter 1

An Elder's Calling

Gary L. Johnson

**"If you are a Christian, then you are a minister.
A non-ministering Christian is a contradiction in terms."**
D. Elton Trueblood

It was 1904 when William Borden graduated from a Chicago high school. Young William was an heir to the Borden Dairy estate, and was already a millionaire. To celebrate his graduation from high school, his parents gave him a trip that took him around the world. As William traveled throughout Europe, the Middle East and Asia, he became painfully aware of the suffering of others. Borden became so emotionally burdened that he wrote to his parents, saying, "I'm going to give my life to prepare for the mission field." At this defining moment in this young man's life, he wrote two words in the back of his Bible: "No reserves."

Borden lived up to those two words as he held nothing back. While attending college at Yale University, Borden became a leader in the Christian community. During his first semester in college, Borden started a small prayer group that grew into a movement on campus, drawing 150 freshmen together for Bible study and prayer every week. By the time Bill Borden was a senior, 1,000 of Yale's then 1,300 students were meeting in such groups on campus. Borden strategically made certain that students heard the good news of Christ while on campus, and he set an example of servant-leadership by reaching out to impoverished people living in New Haven. By graduation from college, the wealthy Borden committed himself to serving among the Muslims living in China. Graduation from Yale was another defining moment in his life, and once again he wrote two words in the back of his Bible. Alongside the words "no reserves," Borden wrote "no retreats."

Borden lived that sentiment. Refusing a number of lucrative job offers, he went to graduate school, and after graduating from seminary, Borden went to Egypt to learn Arabic, as he intended to work among the Muslim Kansu people of China. While in Egypt, he contracted spinal meningitis. Within a month, 25-year-old William Borden was dead. Prior to dying, William Borden had written two more words in his Bible. Alongside the words "No reserves" and "No retreats," Borden wrote: "No regrets."[1]

We, like Borden, want to live spiritually significant lives for the glory of God. Yet, are we—like Borden—willing to write on the tablets of our hearts: "No reserves, no retreats, no regrets"? Have we surrendered our lives to the lordship of Jesus Christ so that we ache to serve Him when He calls us to do so?

The General Call

From the beginning of time, God has been calling out to people. You see, there can be no calling unless there is a Caller. In the Garden of Eden, God "called" to Adam (Genesis 3:9). God was attempting to get Adam's attention.   When we consider that "God does not change like shifting shadows (James 1:17)," it is reasonable to think that God is still calling out to mankind.

One way in which He calls to mankind is for people to become His followers, and this action is referred to as a general call of God. Until the end of measured time, God will continue to call people to come out of "the world of darkness and into His light" (1 Peter 2:9). Even the word "Church" in Greek (*ekklesia*) means "the called out ones." The prefix *ek* means "out" and the remainder of the word is from the word *kaleo*, meaning "to call, summon." So, God issues a general call to people for them to come out of sinful darkness and into His light. When people choose to respond favorably to that general call, they become a part of the Church, the assembly of His called out ones.

The Leadership Call

Once people answer God's general call, people are expected to serve God (Ephesians 2:10, 1 Peter 4:10). One such way that people rve God is in the area of leadership. The Apostle Paul made mention of the spiritual gift of leadership, and when a person has this gift, they are to "govern diligently" (Romans 12:8). Moreover, it appears that God called people to lead.

In Exodus 3, God called to Moses from a burning bush, and it was a call to lead the Israelites out of bondage in Egypt to freedom in the Promised Land. It is interesting to note that it took a burning bush for Moses to turn aside from his hum-drum daily routine; turning his attention to a strange sight. As a shepherd, Moses' work typically resulted in being in a rut—quite literally. Sheep and goats are notorious for walking in the same path. Could it be that Moses was so enamored with his routine that a miracle was needed to cause him to look up, to inquire as to something unique taking place in his life? In this moment, God called Moses into a position of leadership.

Moreover, Moses resisted that calling. Not once, but five times, Moses hesitated in answering God's call to leadership (Exodus 3:11, 13; 4:1, 10, 13). God was not pleased with Moses' response, as His "anger burned against him" (Exodus 4:14). Yet, Moses finally yielded to the will of God for his life, and he answered God's call to lead.

It wasn't a burning bush, but a blinding light that captured the attention of another man. While walking to Damascus, Jesus appeared to Saul in a blinding light and called him to lead (Acts 9:1-22). Saul was a fully-devoted God-follower, but now he was given the opportunity to follow Jesus Christ as his Messiah, and to serve Him as a leader.

God called young Samuel into a leadership role of prophet (1 Samuel 3), and his position as a God-appointed prophet was recognized by the people (verse 20). Jesus called twelve men to be leaders, and these "Apostles"—a word meaning "the ones sent"—were given the mission to lead the way in establishing the first century Church.

Over and again, we can find instances when God called men to lead—and He still does the same today. God is immutable—unchanging—and He calls men to lead His Church. The Apostle Peter urged elders to "serve as overseers—not because you must, but because you are willing, as God wants you to be" (1 Peter 5:2). Are men serving as elders, and doing so just out of a sense of duty? Are men serving as elders because they have been "voted in" by people, as opposed to being called by God? When a man has a desire to serve and experiences a passionate stirring of his soul, God just may be calling him to lead.

Wilson Bentley died pursuing his passion. Wilson was a farm boy from Jericho, Vermont, and while growing up on the farm, he developed a fascination with snowflakes. Simply put, he was obsessed. While most people stay inside during a snowstorm, Bentley did just the opposite. As soon as it started snowing, Bentley ran outside to catch snowflakes on a black velvet cloth. He, then, would examine them under a microscope and photograph them before they melted. He discovered that every snowflake was an individual masterpiece of creation. To preserve the unique design of a snowflake, Bentley took photomicrographs of them, with his first taken on January 15, 1885. Pursuing this passion for over half a century, Bentley produced a collection of 5,381 photographs.

The first known photographer of snowflakes, Wilson pursued his passion for more than fifty years. He amassed a collection of 5,381 photographs that was published in his masterpiece called *Snow Crystals*. Shortly after the publication of his magnum-opus, Bentley died in a manner befitting the artistic genius. On December 23, 1931, Wilson "Snowflake" Bentley died of pneumonia, which he contracted after walking six miles through a blinding snowstorm. Bentley died still pursuing his passion.[2]

Is serving as an elder of the local church a passion in your life? Are you pursuing that passion in an authentic way? While people in the church may be "electing" you to serve, God may be calling you to serve.

☎ **Reflection Question:** If you are serving as an elder, recall the process that led you to this position of service. What words would you use to describe that process?

What does a call to lead look like?

Practically speaking, how can men tell if there is a call of God on their lives to lead? Is it difficult to discern this call? It is interesting to note unique aspects of God's leadership calls to Moses, Paul and Samuel. For example, when God called each of these men to lead, He said their names twice (Exodus 3:4 "Moses, Moses"; 1 Samuel 3:10 "Samuel, Samuel"; Acts 9:4 "Saul, Saul"). Is there something in us as men that we do not hear very well? When growing up, was your name ever repeated when someone attempted to get your attention? Chances are—that did happen—and still does. Moreover, not only does something verbal stand out about these three calls to leadership, but there is something visual. As mentioned earlier, it took a burning bush and a blinding light to get the attention of Moses and Saul. What will it take for God to get us to turn aside to Him should He call? When God called Samuel, he was lying down (1 Samuel 3:3). It was the end of his day, and he was physically still. When will we slow down long enough to sense God's call on our lives? Our frenetic pace of life does not lend itself to hearing God well.

Teens have discovered a ring-tone for their cell phones that work to their advantage. Called the "mosquito tone," this ring is much too high in pitch for adults twenty-five years of age and older to hear. The young people find this ringtone to their liking because parents, teachers, employers, etc. cannot hear it. Typically, people over twenty-five years old cannot hear sounds above 16 kilohertz, and the mosquito tone rings in at 17 Khz.

In much the same way, we have some difficulties in "hearing" God when He calls out to us. Perhaps, our lives are so activity-driven that we cannot sense God's call, or it may be that the pace at which we live life makes little or no room for God. Regretfully, we struggle hearing God's call.[3]

In John MacArthur's *Rediscovering Pastoral Ministry*, James M. George describes a four-step process by which to discern if God's call was upon someone's life for vocational ministry.[4] Being that elders are called to spiritual leadership, there is a good deal of cross-over information from his essay on "The Call to Pastoral Ministry" that is of practical help to us. James George encourages us to use the acronym C.A.L.L. as a memory tool to help sort our thoughts, as we try to determine if God is calling us to serve as elders.

☎ **Reflection Question:** What motivates you to serve as an elder? How deeply do you desire this opportunity?

C for Confirmation: Have people spoken into your life, mentioning that they recognize leadership traits and potential within you? If so, take note that God may be trying to get your attention. In Acts 16:1-2, young Timothy was recruited into the ministry as Paul heard from believers that Timothy was an exceptional young man. A plurality of believers (i.e., both in Lystra and Iconium) spoke well of

Timothy. They affirmed him to Paul. In Proverbs 11:14, we are reminded that "many advisors make victory sure." Are we listening and paying attention to right-minded advisors in our lives? Perhaps, these individuals are being prompted by the Lord to help us consider that God may be calling us to lead His Church.

Not only are we confirmed by the comments of others, but people receive a sense of confirmation from God. If we are being called to lead the Church, God may enable us to experience moments of effective leading without being an actual elder. This "testing of the water" can help us recognize if we have the potential skills necessary for leading in a much more significant manner.

☎ **Reflection Question:** Have people verbally affirmed your potential to serve in as an elder? If so, what do you recall them saying to you?

A for Abilities: Far too often, men are serving as elders who are not skilled in leading. It may be that they have been selected to serve because they are effective businessmen, reputable members of the church and community, etc. Yet, little consideration is given to the issue of their skills. To lead effectively, an elder should have interpersonal skills, be able to communicate effectively, and able to think analytically. An elder should have some skill in communicating the Word, whether that be preaching or teaching Scripture effectively. An elder must be skilled in pastoral care, as well as in administering church discipline. Fundamental leadership skills are needed if we are to have capable elders. When an individual takes an honest look at his spiritual gifting, and realizes he "has what it will take" to serve as an elder, it may be that God is calling him to lead.

Could Moses have taken such an inventory of his life when considering God's call for him to lead? His years spent in Egypt were instrumental, equipping Moses as a capable leader. Having grown

15

up in Egypt, he understood the Egyptian culture and polity. He was well educated, and lived in the royal ranks of Egypt. After leaving Egypt, Moses worked as a shepherd for forty years, where he developed skills for leading a "flock" of people through a wilderness. When we look at our previous educational pursuits, vocational experiences, and Christian service, it may be that we recognize leadership potential within us. Having such abilities may be further evidence that God is calling us to lead.

☎ **Reflection Question:** What abilities do you have that enable you to serve effectively in this role?

L for Longing: If God is calling us to lead, a longing or desire should stir within us. Peter wrote that we are to "desire" this opportunity to serve (see 1 Peter 5:1-2). Desire is longing. Do we ache for the local church to be vibrant in spiritual health, advancing the person of Jesus Christ throughout the community? Do we envision a prevailing, effective ministry that is led in an exceptional, relevant manner? Do such thoughts keep us awake at night or enter our waking thoughts at dawn? When we humbly desire to be a servant-leader of the local church, a longing can indicate a call of God to lead.

Frederick Buechner, U.S. writer and preacher (1926–), once said, "The place God calls you to is the place where your deep gladness and the world's deep hunger meet." Just imagine if each of us, who serve as elders, experienced deep gladness while serving to satisfy the deep hunger of those in the local church. A longing within us can be God's calling to us.

☎ **Reflection Question:** What motives fuel your call to serve effectively as an elder in the Church?

L for Lifestyle: Not everyone has a lifestyle that is conducive to serve as an elder. First and foremost, an elder must be a man of consistent, Christian character. He may possess great credentials and skills, but if he is not a man of moral integrity, he is not being called to lead the local church. A lifestyle that emulates godliness and Christlikeness is mandatory. How is this lifestyle recognized? Men who are genuinely content with what they have, who hunger for holiness, and who are genuinely humble exhibit traits conducive of an appropriate lifestyle for leading the local church. Men who are self-disciplined in their Christian walk, and who are radically devoted to his family, the Church, and the Word exhibit a lifestyle befitting a spiritual leader.

☎ **Reflection Question:** Does your lifestyle enhance or diminish your effectiveness as an elder? Explain.

WHY is it important to sense this call to the leadership ministry?

Leading the local church is difficult and demanding. Regretfully, some men are no longer serving as elders because their ministry was too painful for them. Knowing and sensing that we have been called to serve as elders can strengthen our resolve to continue serving as elders when such work becomes difficult.

In the Old Testament, Jeremiah was called by God to lead. His long-term ministry was far from pleasant. He was constantly under attack and became the brunt of criticism. He suffered so greatly during his forty-plus years of ministry that he earned the nick-name "the weeping prophet." Yet, Jeremiah did not quit for he knew that he had been called by God to lead.

The same was experienced by the Apostle Paul. He was called by Jesus to lead (see Acts 9:15), and suffering became a hallmark of his ministry. It is interesting to trace some of Paul's steps of suffering.

In Acts 16:12, Paul arrived in Philippi, a Roman colony. While there, he healed a young girl who was demon possessed, and that act of kindness resulted in him being "stripped and beaten" in the marketplace (verses 19-22). After his miraculous release from prison, Paul went to Thessalonica (Acts 17:1), but was later driven from that city for simply having preached Jesus Christ (verse 10). Paul then went to Berea, where he was again driven from that city for simply preaching Jesus (verse 14). Paul then went to Athens (verse 16), and on arriving there, he was "greatly distressed" at the sight of all the idols. From there, Paul went to Corinth (Acts 18:1), and it wasn't idolatry that distressed him, it would have been the sexual immorality present in that city. While there, the Lord appeared to Paul in a vision (verse 9) and said, "Do not be afraid; keep on speaking, do not be silent."

Why would the Lord say this to Paul? Could it be that Paul wanted to quit? Could Paul have been so discouraged from the beating and imprisonment in Philippi, and the rejection in Thessalonica and Berea that he wanted to give up? After witnessing idolatry and immorality on epic scales, could Paul have thought, "What's the use?" Was he physically, emotionally and spiritually exhausted to the point of throwing in the proverbial towel? Did it take a supernatural intervention of the Lord to remind Paul of the call on his life? Fortunately for us, Paul did not quit. He stayed faithful to his call to lead.

When we are convinced that God has called us to lead His Church, we are less likely to quit when it becomes difficult to lead. There is great benefit for knowing that we have been called to lead. Author Kirsten Strand describes well what matters when all is said and done.

> I have learned that ignoring a calling can lead to depression, anger, frustration, and a deep dissatisfaction with life. And I have learned that following a calling can also lead to moments

of depression, anger, frustration, and loneliness. Yet, underneath those feelings will be a profound sense of peace and satisfaction.[5]

Answer — and enjoy — His call.

☎ **Group Reflection Questions:**
- What are the common influences to your calling as elders? How do your call's compare?
- As elders, when you are considering someone for the eldership, how do you assess their call to serve?
- How well do you individual abilities fit together into a healthy leadership for the entire congregation?
- How do you encourage one another to have a closer walk with Christ? What tangible engagements do you have with one another beyond the work of elder?

Endnotes

[1]www.preachingtoday.com siting Bill White, Paramount, California; sources: *Daily Bread* (12-31-1988); *The Yale Standard* (Fall 1970); Mrs. Howard Taylor, Borden of Yale (Bethany House, 1988)

[2]Mark Batterson, *Wild Goose Chase* (Sister's, OR: Multnomah, 2008), pp. 15-16.

[3]Doug Newton, "Spiritual Ear Hair," *Light & Life* (January/February 2008), p. 32.

[4]John MacArthur, eds. *Rediscovering PastoralMinistry* (Dallas, TX: Word Publishing, 1995), p. 102f.

[5]Kirsten Strand, "Following a Tough Call," GiftedforLeadership.com (3-31-07).

Chapter 2

Elder Conversion and Transformation

David Roadcup

A prominent church leader recently wrote the following: "The local church is the hope of the world and its future rests primarily in the hands of its leaders."[1] The three authors of this volume heartily agree! We love and serve the church on a full time basis. Our lives are rooted in the church. We live and breathe the church 24-7. We believe in the future and potential of the church. We believe that Jesus is the head of the church. We believe the church to genuinely be the living, breathing body of Jesus Christ. We believe that God created the church to be the vessel which will take believers to heaven. We believe that the church is to be God's collective representative to a world wanting to see authenticity in Christian living. We believe the church will be the Bride of Christ at the Wedding Feast of the Lamb as the Book of Revelation tells us. We believe in the church and are excited about the church's future!

We also deeply appreciate and love elders in congregations. Most of these servants are volunteers who give of their time, effort, energy and gifts to enable, nurture and grow the body of Christ. We salute and appreciate each one!

In light of these admissions, a major point comes to the fore. The clear issue before us is that the future of the church definitely rests in the hands of leadership people. Let me reiterate that the future, effectiveness, accomplishment and results of the life and work of the church rest in the hands of its leaders. These leaders are led by God, graced by the Presence of Jesus our Lord and empowered by the Holy Spirit. In light of this truth, another statement is true: As the leadership of the church goes, so goes the church. In my forty-five years of church leadership, this fact is true: when Godly, competent, effective leaders are at the helm of the church, positive things happen. When people who are leading the church are not committed, incompetent, and lack the leadership gift, the church usually drifts or flounders. This has been true through the centuries, is true now and always will be true. The effectiveness and ability of the church to fulfill its mission depends on several key factors, one of the most important being the effectiveness of each church's paid and volunteer leadership team.

This chapter will deal with the transformation factor in the life of an elder or church leader. Every elder who serves must have experienced the transformation of life that comes from a serious, personal encounter with Jesus Christ and his Word! He must be personally and authentically transformed in his nature. Every elder. growing, well balanced, fruitful church.

☎ **Reflection Question:** On a scale of ① ② ③ ④ ⑤ ⑥ ⑦, low to high, where would you place your spiritual life? Why do you rate yourself in this way?

Jesus Admonition and Call

Scripture clearly explains what the transformation process is in the life of a leader or believer. We want to examine several passages on this topic to glean their content.

The best place to start is with Jesus and his request concerning becoming his disciple. Jesus communicates to us in Luke 9:23-24 what He is asking from us. He says, "If anyone wishes to come after me, he must deny himself, and take up his cross daily and follow me. For whoever wishes to save his life will lose it, but whoever looses his life for my sake, he is the one who will save it."

In this text, Jesus gives us His requirements for discipleship. He asks this; "If there is anyone who is serious about following me, that person must die to themselves, submitting every area of their lives to my Lordship". That is the key concept Jesus is communicating here. A total abandon of self. A dying my own wants and a saying "yes" to the Lord's will and direction for my life. I die to myself to live daily for Jesus.

What Jesus is asking for here is the heart and soul of following Him. He is simply asking for *everything*. Not a few token works of obedience. Everything. All of it. The whole enchilada. The complete package with nothing held back. It is absolutely true that coming to this place in the life of an elder or follower takes time. But, *the decision to make this step*, the mental, psychological, emotional and spiritual "driving of a stake", to make this the goal in my spiritual walk is what Jesus is seeking in His followers. This decision must be sincere. It must come from the heart. It must be completely authentic. It must come from the marrow of our bones. It must come from a broken spirit of repentance. It must originate and continue from the deepest part of our interior world. It must be with us every day. It is the key to our authentic, on-going relationship to Christ. Men of deep, personal, spiritual transformation should be leading our congregations.

At present in the American church, there is a dangerous trend in preaching and teaching. Sometimes without realizing it, we communicate to the people in our churches and say, "If you do three basic things as a Christian, you are home free. First, come to church when there are services. Second, give an offering when the offering is taken. Third, be as morally good as possible. ("Don't embarrass us on the outside"). As people attend our services, it is possible for them to get this muted message as opposed to Jesus' qualification for discipleship. It is important to note that these three issues were not in the core of Jesus' requirements for discipleship. He knew that these three issues (and other important aspects of a spiritually healthy disciple) would be by-products of dying to oneself.

We want to begin with Jesus statement on this important topic. Jesus, himself extends to us the expectation for transformation. His words communicate the clear message to us in Luke 9:23-24. Let's examine verse 23 phrase by phrase to glean its meaning.

"If anyone ..."

There are several key observations that need to be closely examined in this passage. First, Jesus says, "If anyone". We must remember that Jesus is a gentleman. He will never force his way into anyone's life. He is saying here, "You make the decision. It is up to you." So, it is a decision of our intellect, emotions and spirit. We proactively, with serious intent, make the decision to personally invite Jesus Christ to become the One Supreme King and Ruler over the principality of our hearts.

"Wishes to come after me ..."

This is Jesus' specific invitation to become his disciple or follower. Part of this commitment means that we will become like Jesus when we become his disciple. Jesus talked specifically about this in Luke 6:40 when he stated, "A pupil is not above his teacher; but everyone, after he has been fully trained, will be like his teacher." Becoming like Jesus in every area of our lives should be one of the main goals of every Christ follower. Paul teaches about this same point in Ephesians 4:13. He states, "until we all attain to the unity of the faith, and the knowledge of the Son of God, *to a mature man, to the measure of the stature which belongs to the fullness of Christ*." One growing, desire of the heart of every elder or leader who is truly following Christ is the desire to become like Jesus in every way. An incredible compliment in the life of a Christian leader would be for someone to tell him that he reminds them of Jesus.

"He must deny himself . . ."

The heart of the issue here is so clear. Jesus is asking that we be willing to deny ourselves in order to follow Him. Jesus is asking us to make a decision about who will be in control of our lives. It will either be Jesus or ourselves. The act of denying ourselves simply means that we will say no to ourselves and yes to Jesus. We will cease to be in charge of our lives. We are willing to hand over the direction  and control of our lives to Christ. What Jesus is asking us to do is simply this, it is to "Kill our will". He is asking us to nail our wills to our own personal crosses. In doing so, we give to Him control when it comes to our life choices, decisions, time, money, family and futures. The issue is clear. It is the issue of who is ultimately in control of our lives. It must always be Jesus.

This decision is the bedrock of our relationship to Christ. It is key. Dallas Willard observes, "Self-denial must never be confused with self-*rejection*; nor is it to be thought of as a painful and strenuous *act*, perhaps repeated from time to time against great internal resistance. It is, rather, an overall, settled condition of life in the kingdom of God, better described as 'death to self.' In this and in this alone lies the key to the soul's restoration. Christian spiritual formation rests on this indispensable foundation of death to self and cannot proceed except insofar as that foundation is being firmly laid and sustained."[2]

Another significant leader of the church, Dietrich Bonhoeffer, comments about this struggle in his writings; "The disciple must say to himself the same words Peter said of Christ when he denied him: 'I know not this man.' Self-denial is never just a series of isolated acts of mortification or asceticism. It is not suicide, for there is an element of self-will even in that. To deny oneself is to be aware only of Christ and no more of self, to see only him who goes before and no more the road which is too hard for us. Once more, all that self-denial can say is: He leads the way, keep close to him."[3]

C.S. Lewis observed, "The Christian way is different; harder, and easier. Christ says, 'Give me all.' I don't want so much of your time and so much of your money and so much of your work: I want you. I have not come to torment your natural self, but to kill it. No half-measures are any good. I don't want to cut off a branch here and a branch there, I want to have the whole tree down. I don't want to drill the tooth, or crown it, or stop it, but to have it out. Hand over the whole natural self, all the desires which you think innocent as well as the ones you think wicked – the whole outfit. I will give you a new self instead. In fact, I will give you myself: my own will shall become yours."[4] Lewis' point is poignant and clear. He points out that Jesus is asking everything from us.

A leading evangelism ministry has as part of their teaching the idea that there is a throne in every person's life.[5] They have a schematic that depicts two thrones. On one throne is a large "E" representing the concept of a *person's ego*. On a second throne, there is a cross, representing *Christ*.

The question is this: *"In your life, who is on the throne?"* This is the key issue for each of us. Who is reigning supreme? Whose will is in control and what kind of obedience is being produced as a result? There are definitely two entities in contention here – it is either myself or it is Jesus. And this is exactly what Jesus is referring to when he asks us to deny ourselves. It means that I am willingly giving up control to my life to Jesus Christ, knowing and trusting him to perform His will in me in every situation.

As the Christian leader continues to grow in their faith and spiritual life, the concept of and need for dying to oneself become a reality. We see that it is truly what Christ calls for from all of his followers. Dallas Willard puts it well as he states, "But the fact (dying to oneself) that it represents is a fundamental, indispensable element in the renovation of the heart, soul, and life. Being dead to self is the condition where the mere fact that I do not get what I want does not surprise or offend me and has no control over me."[6]

☎ **Reflection Question:** Is there an area of your life in which Christ is not recognizable? While He may be evident throughout your life, is there any area He is not as visible?

"Take up his cross daily and follow me . . ."

Jesus continues by explaining how we kill our will. His statement is vivid and dramatic. He says each person must be willing to "take up his cross daily and follow me". "When Christ calls a man, he bids him come and die."[7] We are called to die to ourselves. He, again, is asking for the death of our will when it comes to who is in control of our lives.

One of the things we can love about Jesus is that he never asks us to do anything that he was not willing to do, first, himself. Jesus calls us to crucify ourselves in order to become his followers. He then goes first, before us as our example, and shows us how it is done. Vernon Grounds writes concerning the "Gethsemane mind-set" (that attitude demonstrated by Jesus Christ on the night of His betrayal).[8] Jesus attitude was that he was willing to die on the cross for our salvation. We must be ready to die to ourselves to become authentic disciples in following our Lord, who gave us the example. Jesus always sets the pace.

The apostle Paul understood this concept clearly. He writes, "I have been crucified with Christ, and it is no longer I who live, but Christ lives in me; and the life which I now live in the flesh I now live by faith in the Son of God, who loved me and delivered Himself up for me." (Gal. 2:20) Paul again states, "But may it never be that I should boast, except in the cross of our Lord Jesus Christ, through which the world has been crucified to me, and I to the world." (Galatians 6:14)

About us, he states, "Now those who belong to Christ Jesus have crucified the flesh with its passions and desires." (Gal. 5:24). In Romans 6:6, Paul says "Knowing this, that our old self was crucified with Him, that our body of sin might be done away with, that we should no longer be slaves to sin."

Jesus modeled for us what he would be asking us to do. The Apostle Paul understood and wrote to remind us of this concept. We are clearly called to follow Jesus and obey his request.

A very important question at this juncture is this, "Did the people listening to Jesus' teaching understand what he meant when he said, "take up your cross"? History would tell us that they did. We know that crucifixion began around 200 years before the time of Christ. It is thought that the Carthaginians or the Phoenicians started the practice. By Jesus' time, the Romans had brought this death practice to an all time level of pain and torture. Without question, Jesus knew of this practice. In an article titled, "The Way of the

Cross", author Skip Grey writes, "Tradition tells us that when Jesus was a teenager, there was a rebellion by Jews near where he lived. The Roman army crushed the rebellion and to teach Jews a lesson, crucified an Israelite every ten meters along a road for the distance of 16 kilometers. The sight of some 1,760 people dead or dying in agony, on crosses spaced every 30 feet for 10 miles must have made an indelible impression on the mind of a teenager. Long before his death, the cross was an ugly hideous reality.[9]

Jesus is calling us to die. We say "Yes" to Jesus and "No" to ourselves. For anyone, this is not natural or easy but is the move that allows us to fulfill Jesus' request in our lives.

In our day and time, we may have a little trouble identifying with this penetrating request of Jesus. In our cultural parlance today, Jesus might say to us, "If anyone wishes to follow me, he must strap himself into his own electric chair and throw the switch." Or, he may say, "If you want to follow  me, you must lay down on a gurney, insert the IVs for your own lethal injection and push the plunger yourself." This request may appear shocking to us, but Jesus request to kill our will is absolutely necessary. There cannot be two entities leading our lives. It must come down to Jesus as both Savior and Lord of our lives.

A.W. Tozer has a powerful observation in his writings concerning the topic.[10] Tozer says there are three marks of a person who has been crucified:

1. *He is facing in only one direction.* Jesus redefines the focus of our lives. We have one passion and purpose, which is to know and serve Christ. The priorities of God become our priorities. We give ourselves up to serve and advance Christ. We are now focused in one direction.

2. *He can never turn back.* Nowhere in recorded history is there an example of someone who experienced the initial act of crucifixion and was then taken down from their cross alive. Crucifixion was always permanent. Jesus said, "And no man, having put his hand to the plow and looking back, is fit for the Kingdom of God. (Luke 9:62) The old camp song is appropriate here – "I have decided to follow Jesus, no turning back, no turning back."

3. *He no longer has any plans of his own.* The person involved no longer has any plans of his own because he no longer belongs to himself. The Lord's plans become our plans. The Lord's agenda, affections and direction become ours. One of our main, daily prayers becomes "Your will be done in my life, Lord. Not mine, but yours."

How do we respond to this request of our Lord? How do make this happen? How does this hard request from our Master become reality in our lives?

The following observations should be made concerning the issue: First, we understand that what Jesus is asking from us is a very difficult to internalize and accomplish. It is not easy for us to will our own wills into death. It definitely takes a decision of our intellect, will and emotions to make this happen. But deciding to make that move is the key. Deciding to decide that I will obey Christ. It comes down to a proactive choice of our intellect and emotions to make the move to follow Jesus in this request.

Second, we realize that it takes time to fully accomplish this request. The decision to follow Christ in this way can be made in an instant. The accomplishment of this task definitely takes much longer. In his book, *You Gotta Keep Dancin'*, Tim Hansel writes, "When I was young in the faith and struggling with the concept of being crucified with Christ, I asked a saintly, elderly woman, 'Why, if my old nature has been crucified with Christ, does it continue to keep on wiggling?' She smiled and in a quiet voice, said, 'You must remember, Tim, that crucifixion is a slow death.'"[11]

Dallas Willard reminds us, "The 'interior castle' of the human soul has many rooms, and they are slowly occupied by God, allowing us time and room to grow.'"[12]

Third, there is help for us in fulfilling Jesus' request. Jesus did not leave us without assistance. He daily sends us help and encouragement through the ministry of the Holy Spirit and His presence in our lives. Jesus told us, "I will ask the Father, and he will give you another Helper, that He may be with you forever; that is the Spirit of truth, whom the world cannot receive, because it does not see Him or know Him, but you know Him because He abides with you and will be in you. (John 14:16-17)

The fellow Christians who make up our church family and other believers we know can also be a great help in providing encouragement, support and motivation as we move along on our individual journeys.

 George Muller, one of the spiritual giants of yesteryear, tells of his personal journey in following Christ. Muller writes, "I became a believer in the Lord Jesus in the beginning of November, 1825 …………. For the first four years afterward, it was for a good part in great weakness; but in July 1829 ………….. it came to me to an entire and full surrender of heart. I gave myself fully to the Lord. Honor, pleasure, money, my physical powers, my mental powers, all was laid down at the feet of Jesus, and I became a great lover of the Word of God. I found my all in God." Someone asked him the secret of his service for God. He replied, "There was a day when I died, utterly died; died to George Muller, his opinions,

preferences, tastes and will—died to the world, its approval or censure, died to the approval or blame even of my brethren and friends – and since then I have studied to show myself approved unto God."[13]

God is calling every leader who leads his church to grow in the area of becoming fully committed, of experiencing personal, spiritual transformation. This is not an easy calling but one which is absolutely necessary for leaders to possess. God knows this process takes time. God is not calling us to perfection. He knows we can never attain perfection. But He is calling us to maturity and growth.

We should also point out that Jesus gives this request, mentioning its frequency. When he includes the word, "daily", we see the time table of the request. Jesus is not calling us to die to ourselves once a year, once a month once a week. For the authentic follower, it is definitely a *daily* thing. It becomes part of our daily life and existence.

So Jesus' request is clear. He is saying to each of us, "If you are truly serious about becoming my disciple, you must decide to die to yourself and live each day for me. Nothing short of this is acceptable in becoming my disciple."

Paul's Exhortation

Paul, also illumines this teaching of Jesus as he pens Romans 12:1-2. This text carefully describes the transformation process. Paul writes and states, "Therefore I urge you, brethren, by the mercies of God, to present your bodies a living and holy sacrifice, acceptable to God, which is your spiritual service of worship. And do not be conformed to this world but be transformed by the renewing of your mind, so that you may prove what the will of God is, that which is good and acceptable and perfect."

Paul states clearly that when a person comes to belief in Jesus as the Christ, experiences genuine repentance from sin and receives Christian baptism, a new life is formed in that believer. A spiritual transformation should take place in that person's life. The word used in the original language in Rom. 12:2 for "transformation" is the word *metamorphousthe*. We recognize a derivative of this word, metamorphosis from high school biology class. It is the description of a caterpillar entering a cocoon, fulfilling the gestation period and emerging a beautiful butterfly. A truly amazing work of nature! Tadpoles into frogs and other miracles of science take place as metamorphosis happens. It's interesting that Paul would use this word to describe what happens when a believer becomes a Christian. The key is this – just as there is a change in the nature of a caterpillar as it becomes a butterfly, there should be a change in the nature of a person as they become a Christian. There should be a change in a believer's nature. There is little change on the outside. The miraculous change is on the inside. This beautiful word picture given to us by Paul makes the picture clear. It is definitely part of the experience of a believer coming to Jesus. When we genuinely come to Christ, our nature changes to reflect the mind of Jesus in our lives.

In 2 Corinthians 5:17 Paul adds yet another point of clarification when he reminds us, "Therefore if anyone is in Christ, he is a new creature; the old things passed away; behold, new things have come." Paul is reminding us that our new life in Christ involves a change for the better. After Christ, we are not the same. The old is gone. The new has arrived.

☎ **Reflection Question:** Can you think of any action steps you can do to start an even closer walk with Jesus Christ?

Applying What We Know

Now why this extended treatise on transformation in a book on church elders and leaders? The issue is this: You may find it interesting that students of evangelism have identified classifications of people who need to be reached with the gospel. They are identified in the following manner:

E-1 - Evangelism which reaches people who are geographically near and of similar culture to the congregation.

E-2 - Evangelism which crosses ethnic, cultural and class barriers.

E-3 – Evangelism which crosses linguistic barriers.

E-0 - Evangelism which reaches the unconverted members of the congregation.[14]

This type of evangelism is also called "Intra-evangelism". People seeking to be reached are sometimes called "notional members". These are folks who attend services and would count themselves active participants of the activities and ministries of the church. The true situation is, while being active and attending services, they have never undergone an authentic conversion experience, having been transformed in their interior worlds. George Barna's research tells us that in today's typical congregation, approximately 44% of all adult Americans who participate in church life are unconverted![15] Jesus also faced this dilemma as he encountered spiritual leaders, Pharisees and Saducees, who wore the robes of righteousness and ministered in the Temple but were far away from God in their interior worlds. Paul also warns about this difficulty in Philippians 1:15-18. Men in his sphere of relationships were ministering in the name of Christ with impure motives, envy and strife.   The problem is not new, and is still prevalent today, being found widely in the life of the Church.

In light of this truth, local congregations may have the tendency to place people into key leadership positions who fall into the category of notional members. Some churches may see the issue of "holding church membership" or simply "going to church" as evidence enough that someone is qualified to lead as an elder. Although very aware of Scriptural guidelines, churches sometimes place people in leadership roles because they are successful in business, have ordered families, attend church services regularly and donate financially to the church's cause. While each of these points is desirable and evidence of good things in the life of the attendee, these elements, alone, may not cover the foundational point of genuine conversion and personal transformation. Therefore, people who have never experienced the transforming power of dying to themselves in obedience to Christ are made elders or placed in influential positions. In doing so, they obtain major influence in the life and direction of a church. People may be placed into elder positions who may not have a Christian world view, do not really know Scriptural teaching about many issues or who have not developed the mind of Christ. Carnal Christians who are put into key leadership positions will not lead the church with the mind and heart of Jesus. The problems, difficulties and struggles which result can be devastating. This can be one of the explanations for the unchristian behavior, carnal actions and harsh decisions of some people who are presently in the role of elder or minister. Ego issues, the need for prominence and control resulting in power struggles, a lack of love, patience and forbearance in the midst of flaring tempers sometimes present themselves in leadership settings. Friends, this behavior and activity should not be found in the leadership (or followership) of the Body of Christ!

Let me make this point with great clarity: It's not that those placed in the role of elder must be perfect. *Quite the opposite.* If that were the case, no one would be an elder. God is not calling us to perfection but in the case of those who lead the church, God is calling them to maturity and depth of spirit. They are called to strong, spiritual leadership based in the Holy Spirit. This is exactly why Paul tells Timothy not to install new believers into eldership roles.

The point is then clear. Every person who makes up the spiritual leadership team of a church should be living transformed lives. They are people who know Jesus deeply and are crucifying themselves daily. They understand that living for Jesus in authenticity is the heart of being in the harness in leadership. For a person to become an elder, he must have encountered the living Christ, heard his call to authentic discipleship and must be seeking to live the crucified life with the help of the Holy Spirit. If a man is found to not be seeking Christ in this way, he should definitely review his call to lead. If a man is presently serving as an elder and is not struggling to die to himself, he should consider resigning his leadership role until he has made the proactive decision to follow Christ at this level. Teaching, support, encouragement and love should be extended by the church to all men who are in leadership roles. They should regularly be lifted up in prayer, supported and encouraged. Patience, forbearance and grace should be extended to all leaders who are truly moving closer to Christ as their spiritual journeys progress.

In light of what Jesus calls for when it comes to a transformed life, can people who are in the main leadership roles of the body of Christ possess anything less? Let us band together as leaders and pursue Jesus, living transformed lives with all of our hearts!

☎ **Reflection Question:** Where did this chapter "step on your toes"?

☎ **Reflection Question:** What life-change may this chapter have compelled you to make?

☎ **Group Reflection Questions**
- How do we, as elders, promote the spiritual growth of one another?
- As elders, are there any matters or dealings of which we should repent?
- Where can we exemplify Christ more in our role as elders?
- As an eldership, how can we better develop a real sense of accountability and encouragement?

Endnotes

[1] Bill Hybels, *Courageous Leadership* (Grand Rapids, Michigan: Zondervan, 2002), p. 27.
[2] Dallas Willard, *Renovation of the Heart : Putting on the Character of Christ* (Colorado Springs, Colorado: NavPress Group, 2004), p. 64.
[3] Dietrich Bonhoeffer, *The Cost of Discipleship* (New York: The Macmillan Company, 1969), p. 97.
[4] C.S.Lewis, *Mere Christianity* (New York: HarperCollins, 2001), pp.196-197.

[5] This illustration was originally made by Campus Crusade for Christ and has since been used formally and informally as a means of opening evangelistic conversations.

[6] Willard, *Renovation of the Heart*, p. 71.

[7] Bonhoeffer, *The Cost of Discipleship*, p. 99.

[8] Vernon Grounds, *Radical Commitment* (Portland, Origon: Multnoman Press, 1984), p. 41.

[9] Skip Grey, "The Way of the Cross," *Discipleship Journal* 31, (1986) : 6

[10] A.W.Tozer, "Total Commitment to Christ", American Gospel Missions Home Page [web site]; accessed 21 October 2008; available from http://www.gospeljohn.com/tozer_commitment.htm.

[11] Tim Hansel, *You Gotta Keep Dancin'* (Elgin, Illinois: David C. Cook Publishing Co, 1985), p. 127.

[12] Dallas Willard, *The Divine Conspiracy : Rediscovering Our Hidden Life in God*. (New York: Harper San Francisco, 1998), p. 30.

[13] Roger Steer, "Seeking First the Kingdom: The Secret of George Muller's Spiritual Peace," *Discipleship Journal* 31, (1986) : 24

[14] Joe Ellis, "Get Real, Church: Becoming a Fully Functional Authentic Biblical Community," Unpublished Manuscript (2003), ch.7, p.2.

[15] George Barna, "Lost in Church: Reaching Churchgoers and National Christians Through Inra-Evangelism." Intra-Evangelism Home Page [web site]; accessed 21 October, 2008; available from http://facingforever.org/

Chapter 3

Biblical Qualities of an Elder

James Riley Estep, Jr.

We all understand that God calls leaders to serve and guide the congregation, but called to *be* what? Calling is more than just task oriented; it is being called to become something. Scripture admonishes that an elder serves "not because you must, but because you are willing, *as God wants you to be*" (1 Pet. 5:2, emphasis added) and is one who "sets his heart on being an overseer, he desires a noble task" (1 Tim. 3:1). God calls individuals who are not only able, but also willing to respond favorably to Him. God can still use a reluctant leader, and many of the Bible's most notable leaders began with an instance of indecision and reluctance to God's call: Moses, Joshua, Jonah, Jeremiah, even Paul! An elder is one who has submitted his life to the call of Jesus Christ to serve as a leader within the congregation, and has the life qualities demonstrating his conversion and transformation.

As one elder expressed during a time of highly volatile church conflict, "Sometimes you want to be an elder, and other times you know God wants you to want to be an elder."[1] It is not enough to simply want to be an elder; he has to possess the basic expectations for an elder as described in Scripture. When someone has the biblical life qualities for leadership, he is equipped to assume the role of an elder. This chapter is not intended to be an exhaustive exegesis of the biblical qualifications for elder, which can be provided by numerous commentaries, nor does it endeavor to definitively outline the essential tasks of an elder or to debate church organization. Rather, it will simply ask the question, "Biblically, what are the biblical expectations of an elder?" To answer this we will look at 1 Timothy,

Titus, and 1 Peter for answers, focusing attention on the call for an elder to be *blameless*.[2]

☎ **Reflection Question:** Can you think of a time during your tenure as an elder that you too have felt this way? How did make your way through the situation? How did it shape your understanding of what it meant to be an elder?

The Essential Quality: *"Blameless"*

The late President Ronald Reagan is best remembered by the title, "The Great Communicator," but perhaps more appropriate in this instance is his title, "The Teflon President." Nothing could stick to him! He was indeed not perfect, and even acknowledged his errors of judgment or mistakes, assuming responsibility and even asking for the country's forgiveness; but accusations of impropriety or questions of his character *simply never stuck*. This is the quality that God desires in an elder. Paul writes that "the overseer must be above reproach" (1 Tim. 3:2) and again that, "An elder must be blameless" (Titus 1:6). While Paul does make use of two different words to describe this quality of a congregational leader, both convey the same essential idea: the person is *unrebukable* or *unaccusable* . . . nothing sticks to them!

Consider this: You select men to serve as candidates for the eldership in your congregation. Before you approve them as elders, you inform the congregation of those who are on the list for their consideration. You are standing before the crowded sanctuary or fellowship hall, preparing to announce the list of candidates. As you read off several of the names, you notice smiles, some applause, perhaps laughter, one man shouts "amen" . . . but when you read off one of the names, there is not only a hush, but a gasp, the sound of murmurs, whispers. Later, you are approached by several individuals who question his inclusion on the list, raising suspicions of poor motive, wrong doing, and questionable beliefs. Regardless of what may be said of the candidate, their ability to serve as a *blameless* leader, one who will not draw suspicion or create distraction for the congregation's leadership, is not apparent. Do you remember Paul's rebuke to the Corinthian congregation in 1 Corinthians 5:1? "It is actually reported that there is sexual immorality among you, and of a kind that *does not occur even among pagans*" (*emphasis added*). Blamelessness is not only a concern for the leader within the church, but even within the community in which the church serves. If an elder is not blameless, they cannot effectively lead the congregation nor can they be a witness to the community for Christ and His church.

Check-sheet or Life Character?

There is more to becoming an elder than simply wanting to serve. When Paul penned his first epistle Timothy and Titus, and Peter wrote his first epistle, they provided a snapshot, a description of what an elder should be. But how are we to approach these lists? While the lists bare strong resemblance to one another, even paralleling one another on occasion, none of these three are identical (Appendix 3.1).

In fact, most commentators agree that Paul's lists share much in common with a list describing the qualifications of a city official or even a military general in ancient Roman culture.[3] The main concern of these qualities is that an elder be blameless, able to serve as an example to the church, and above the reproach of Christians and non-Christians. The list of life qualities provided simply explains the ideal of blamelessness, as if to say "you know what a blameless person looks like, don't you? They are . . ."

Before concerning ourselves with the specific nature of each leadership quality contained within the lists, we must ask several questions that are critical to making the appropriate application of these qualifications, particularly in regard to the "husband of one wife" item.[4]

- *What is the proper biblical meaning of the listed qualification?* What does it really mean to be "not given to drunkenness," "the husband of one wife," or "quick tempered". Does this mean an elder can drink, but just not be drunk? Does it mean that an elder must be married, should you remove widowers from the eldership? If he is passionate about injustice, does this equal quick tempered? Until the meaning of these qualifications are agreed upon by the eldership and congregation, it will be virtually impossible to make beneficial use of the biblical qualifications.

- *Do we consistently apply all the qualification?* If all the qualifications are held to be of equal value and weight, do we apply them consistently as such? Are there one or two qualifications that trump the others? For example, someone is generally angry, known as a grouch, but tolerable; whereas someone else is known for fervently wanting to serve, but has only been a Christian for two years. Should not both be disqualified, or are allowances made for both?

- *How does this qualification reflect the idea of being above reproach?* The central, overarching qualification is blamelessness. How each of these life qualities relates to that central ideal is critical to properly understand them. If a candidate is approached for elder consideration, and he says, "But I am not that great of a teacher." Yet, others in the congregation have shared how much they value his Sunday school lessons, he does indeed have the respect of the congregation and would be regarded as blameless by them, even if he is more critical of his teaching abilities.

- *What if the infraction occurred prior to their conversion?* What if someone had committed a financial crime twenty years ago, went to jail. After his release, he became a Christian, and has been "above reproach" financially ever since? Would he be qualified to serve as an elder? What about a man who was divorced prior to being a Christian, has remarried, and now has an exemplary family in the congregation and community? Would this be held against him?

- *What if a person had a biblically acceptable reason for a given action?* Particularly in the instance of "husband of one wife," if we do maintain that this is a qualification excluding divorced men from serving as an elder,[5] what it was due to the wife's adultery or abandonment? What if it was indeed a case, similar to the situation in 1 Corinthians 7, of a divorce resulting from faith incompatibilities after the husband converted to Christianity, while the wife remained outside the faith? Perhaps the matter of *motive* should be examined and not mere action.

Above all, we must avoid the extreme of *perfectionism*, which can only lead to either spiritual frustration or pharisaic legalism. None of us can read these lists and say, "I embody these qualities 100% of the time in every situation without fault or excuse." *We are not sinless!* That is not what God is expecting, since He is well aware of shortcomings. Rather, is this individual above reproach so as to serve as an example to the congregation and a witness to the community? That is the central issue!

☎ **Reflection Question:** Have you ever battled with perfectionism? How do you balance the call to "blamelessness" and acknowledging your own human faults?

Making Sense of Elder Qualities

God's call to blameless leadership is reflected in the list of qualities for the elder. Paul and Peter both express a concern or the blamelessness of elders and this is reflected in their expectations for the eldership. The biblical expectation to be blameless has several dimensions. It is not simply a matter of personal assessment of one's own character, desires, or abilities; but rather one's call to serve blamelessly before God, others, family, and self (Figure 2.1).

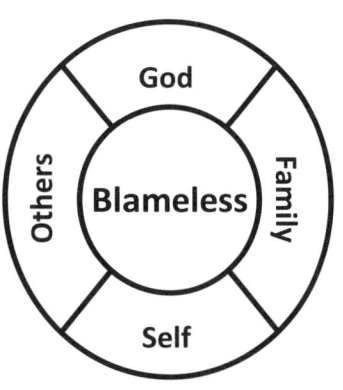

Figure 2.1

The Expectation to be Blameless before God. How would you assess your relationship with God? While indeed no one is perfect, and indeed we could all say with Paul, "I do not set aside the grace of God" (Gal. 2:21), do I have a personal, honest, sincere relationship with Him? This dimension of blamelessness is best reflected in several of the desired qualities of an elder. Peter expresses this best when he writes, that an elder (shepherd) must be capable of being affirmed by the Chief Shepherd (1 Peter 5:4). Elders must have a theological blamelessness before God. For example, he must be one who is "holding firmly to scriptural truths" (Titus 1:9), be able to teach the truth (1 Tim. 3:2, 5:17; 1 Pet. 5:2). He must also be "upright and holy" (Titus 1:8), have a godly motive for desiring to serve as an elder (1 Pet. 5:2), and loving what is good in God's sight (Titus 1:8). Since part of blamelessness requires a mature relationship with God, Paul reminds us that an elder is "not a new covert" (1 Tim. 3:6). Being a blameless leader assumes that our relationship with God is mature, spiritual. Paul's critique of the Corinthian church, "Brothers, I could not address you as spiritual but as worldly — mere infants in Christ" (1 Cor. 3:1) must never apply to elders. We cannot lead others to a mature faith in Christ if we first do not possess it. God expects a congregation's leaders to be blameless before Him.

☎ **Reflection Question:** *Blameless before God*: Identify five terms that best describe your relationship with God:

① _____

② _____

③ _____

④ _____

⑤ _____

In what ways could you improve your relationship with God?

The Expectation to be Blameless before Others: During election years (which are ever two years in the United States), the question of "vetting" is raised. Before being put forward as a candidate for public office, their past and present are examined, the candidate is interviewed, questioned, almost to the point of inquisition; all for the purpose of assuring that they are readily qualified to be presented as a candidate for public office. The general purpose of the vetting process is to assure the character of the individual does not conflict with the office to which they aspire.

What do others say about you? How blameless are your interactions with individuals in the church? In the community? This concern is to a large extent a matter of interpersonal character. Spiritual relationships exist both vertically and horizontally. God's expectation for blamelessness is not only about relating to a forgiving and merciful God, but also to be recognized for one quality of character before others, both within the congregation and to the community outside. Can the individual be presented to the congregation as a blameless leader? Can the community vouch for him? As Paul says, "He must also have a good reputation with outsiders, so that he will not fall into disgrace and into the devil's trap" (1 Tim. 3:7).

Scripture describes such an individual in several ways, all of which explain how an elder is to relate to those he leads and serves. An elder is to be "sincere" (1 Tim. 3:8), "respectable" (1 Tim. 3:2, 8), "hospitable" 1 Tim. 3:2; Titus 1:8), "not quarrelsome" (1 Tim. 3:3), "not violent," rather he is "gentle" (1 Tim. 3:3, Titus 1:7), a man of "good reputation" and an "example" to others (1 Tim. 3:7, 1 Pet. 5:3), "not Overbearing" (Titus 1:7; 1 Pet. 5:3), nor a "pursuer of dishonest gain"(1 Tim. 3:8, Titus 1:7, 1 Pet. 5:2). Such an individual as this could be presented to a congregation without reservation, but also lead the congregation during difficult times through the compulsion of their character. God expects us to be blameless before God's people as well as before those outside the community of faith.

☎ **Reflection Question:** *Blameless before Others:*
If your minister were to talk to those with whom you work, how would they describe you? What concerns might you have about your minister seeing you in a non-church context?

The Expectation to be Blameless before Family: What to those who are closest to you think of you? Your immediate social context is your family. You may be blameless before others who only see you on occasion or for brief vignettes; but what those who share a home with you? How do those with whom you live view your character and call to serve as a leader? How consistent is your commitment to Christ in front of your wife? What about your son or daughter?

Paul identifies three qualities of family life for the elder. *First,* he must be "the husband of but one wife" (1 Tim. 3:2; Titus 1:6). In regard to call, are you blameless in your marriage relationship? Are you blameless where women are concerned? This quality will be fully explored in another volume, but the general condition described by Paul that the elder has the reputation of faithfulness to one woman. How faithful would your wife regard you?[6]

Second, an elder must have believing and obedient children (1Tim. 3:4-5; Titus 1:6). In fact, even his children are to possess the quality of blamelessness, "not open to the charge of being wild and disobedient" (Titus 1:6). Notice Paul's concern for the reputation of the elder, that his family is not "open to the charge" . . . blameless. How blameless are you before your children? This does not mean how perfect a father you are. Rather, how well do you exemplify a growing relationship with Christ before your children? In addition, Paul does explain that Christian "Fathers, do not exasperate your children; instead, bring them up in the training and instruction of the Lord" (Eph. 6:4). We are expected to be blameless, not perfect, before our children, and through our children. This does not mean our children always agree with us, or that our children are perfect examples; but rather that our children regard us to be mature Christians, not a detriment to their faith.

Third, an elder must manage his family well (1 Tim. 3:4; Titus 1:6). Paul adds a rhetorical question, "If anyone does not know how to manage his own family, how can he take care of God's church?" (1 Tim. 3:6). How orderly is your household? Commentators differ on the specific intention of this quality, but the general theme is the orderliness of the household, which could include financial considerations, but it is probably more than this dimension of the household. The simple fact is that a disorderly household can be a manageable distraction for a leader. It is manageable because as the husband of the family you can intervene and bring a sense of order to the household. Failure to do so . . . what will you bring to the church?

☎ **Reflection Question:** *Blameless before Family:*
- Identify something you can do to improve your Christian witness to your wife.
- Identify something you can do to improve your Christian witness to your children.
- Identify something you can do to improve the orderliness to your household.

The Expectation to be Blameless before Self: Have you ever *not* been able to live with yourself? Psychologists talk about the impact of guilt and shame on the self-esteem of individuals. This is not narcissism, a love-of-self to the point of sinful egocentrism. Rather, when you reflect back on your life, do you see a life that reflects positive values and healthy self-image? No hidden secrets? No unresolved or debilitating secrets? Are you responsibly "in control" of your life? *Do you see yourself as blameless?*

Paul identifies several *internal* qualities of an elder. Elders must be "temperate" (1 Tim. 3:2, 8; Titus 1:7), "disciplined" (Titus 1:8), and "self controlled" (1 Tim. 3:2; Titus 1:8); all admirable qualities in a leader. Likewise, Paul calls elders to *not be* "a lover of money" (1 Tim. 3:3), "quick-tempered" (Titus 1:7), or "given to drunkenness" (1 Tim. 3:3, 8; Titus 1:7). A cursory review of these qualities can see the balance. The internal qualities are just that, qualities that are possessed by the individual. The "not" list involves turning our life over to externals, such as money, alcohol, and reactionary responses to threats. [Many psychologists regard anger or temper to be a reaction to a perceived external threat.[7]]

If we are to live blameless lives, we must be *thermostats*, not *thermometers*. Thermostats have an internal control, whereas thermometers simply react to the external environment. To be blameless before self, we must be temperate, disciplines, and self controlled; not simply living in reaction to external stimuli. A

Christian leader must have the thermostatic control of his life centered on Christ, not worldly distractions. *We are called to be blameless to self.*

 Reflection Question: *Blameless before Self:*
You may not want to write this down, but think of one thing you hope no one ever finds out about you. How do you deal with this? How could you deal with this?

Qualities and the Call to be an "Eldership"

Elders do not serve alone. We serve as part of a body of leaders who have all sensed God's call and desired to serve in response to it. The congregation is not led by an elder, or even multiple individuals working independently from one another. Rather, the congregation is led by the collective body of elders, the eldership.

This is indeed God's design for church governance. Paul did not appoint *an* elder over each church, but "elders for them in each church" (Acts 14:23) and even told Titus to "elders in every town, as I directed you" (Titus 1:5). Peter too writes, "To the *elders* among you, I appeal as a *fellow elder,* ..." (1 Pet. 5:1). Elders do not lead alone.

So, what does this have to do with the expected qualities of an elder? *First,* it is important to realize that you are not the only one qualified to serve as an elder. We may differ with others around the table, and may hold differing opinions, but ultimately we realize that God values each individual who matches His expectations of serving "above reproach." *Second,* no one elder possess the quality of blamelessness with all its dimensions to their fullest as described above. However, as an *eldership,* the call to blamelessness is more completely realized. We all bring to the table our strengths and weaknesses, and we complete one another as a leadership. *Third,* we are to exercise servant leadership. An elder must recognize that he did not *earn* the office, nor did he *politic* to attain the office, but rather was summoned by God to serve as a shepherd to His flock, and that one does not serve simply because of an election or personal appointment of a pastor. Your qualification as an elder should not promote the idea of superiority or rank, since that alone would violate the notion of "not lording" over God's people, but "eager to serve" them (1 Peter 5:3).

Reflection Question: *The Eldership:*
How does your eldership, as a body of leaders within the congregation, embody the four dimensions of blamelessness? What do you bring to the table as a leader?

Dimension	Comments
God	
Others	
Family	
Self	

The Qualities of Elders

Leonard Sweet wrote the book *Summoned to Lead* to re-introduce the idea of call into the model of Christian leadership.[8] With so many people describing leadership as vision-casting, an eye metaphor; Sweet reminds the reader that God's metaphor is an ear metaphor. One is *called* into His service. The qualities described in Scripture enable one to not only respond favorably to God's call, but also serve the congregation as a leader. God expects an elder to be blameless before Him, in their witness to others, in their family relations, and even to themselves. We sit at the table of leadership not simply because of a horizontal recognition from within the congregation, but a vertical recognition by God to be a servant to Him in His people.

Endnotes

[1] Anonymous, elder who served at me in a congregation while going through a very difficult episode in the congregation's history.

[2] It should be noted that some commentators regard the use of the term "elder" in 1 Peter is not in reference to the office of elder in the church, but rather the more general use of the term "elder" as in reference to an older individual, similar to the use of "senior" today.

[3] Cf. Burton Scott Easton, *The Pastoral Epistles* (New York: Charles Scribner's Sons, 1947), pp. 83-84, 130-131; Martin Dibelius and Hans Conzelmann, *The Pastoral Epistles* (Philadelphia: Fortress Press, 1972), pp. 50-57; Anthony Tyrrell Hanson, *The Pastoral Letters* (Cambridge: University Press, 1966), pp. 39-40, 109.

[4] James Riley Estep, Jr., "Can the Divorced Man be the 'Husband of One Wife'?," *Christian Standard* (April 18, 1993), pp. 14-16.

[5] It should be noted that since the inception of the church six distinct interpretations of the phrase "husband of one wife" have been present. (1) *Absolute monogamy*, that even after the death of one's wife, he refused to remarry and remained faithful to his one wife; (2) Anti-Digamy, similar to the first, but allowing a man to remarry after the death of his wife; (3) Anti-divorce, which is the most commonly held idea, but certainly not the earliest interpretation and it should be noted that the word for *divorce* while known to Paul is not used in either 1 Timothy or Titus; (4) Anti-polygamy was a common interpretation in the early church, requiring the elder to uphold Jewish, Christian, and even Roman moral tenets; (5) Faithful to one wife focuses on the quality of the marriage, not just the marital status, requiring an elder to have a good reputation where women are concerned, and finally (6) the qualification could simply mean the

elder must be married. All these interpretation are echoed from the early church through today. See Estep, "Can the Divorced Man be the 'Husband of One Wife'?," pp. 14-15.

[6] I understand this qualification to require those in congregational leadership to exhibit a good reputation where women are concerned. I believe it speaks to the quality of a man's character, not a structural consideration of the composition of his family or marital status.

[7] Cf. Andrew D. Lester, *Coping with Your Anger: A Christian Guide* (Philadelphia: Westminster Press, 1983).

[8] Leonard Sweet, *Summoned to Lead* (Grand Rapids: Zondervan Publishing Company, 2004).

Appendix 3.1: Lists of Elder Qualities

1 Timothy 3:1-7	Titus 1:6-9	1 Peter 5:1-4
• *Above reproach (v. 2)* • *Husband of but one wife (v. 2)* • *Temperate (v. 2)*	• *Blameless (v. 6, 7)* • *Husband of but one wife (v. 6)* • Not quick tempered (v. 7)	• *Examples to the flock (v. 4)*
• *Self-controlled (v. 2)* • Respectable (v. 2) • *Hospitable (v. 2)* • Able to Teach (v. 2) • *Not given to drunkenness (v. 3)* • *Not violent,* but gentle (v. 3) • Not quarrelsome (v. 3) • *Not a lover of money (v. 3)*	• *Self-controlled (v. 8)* • *Hospitable (v. 8)* • *Not given to drunkenness (v. 7)* • *Not violent (v. 7)* • *Not given to dishonest gain (v. 7)*	• *Not greedy for money (v. 2)*
• Manage his own family well (v. 4) • *See that his children obey him with proper respect (v. 4, 5)* • Not a recent convert (v. 6) • Good reputation with outsiders (v. 7)	• Children believe and are not open to the charge of being wild and disobedient (v. 6)	
	• Loves what is good (v. 8) • Upright (v. 8) • Holy (v. 8) • Disciplined (v. 8) • He must hold firmly to the trustworthy message as it has been taught (v. 9)	
		• Eager to serve (v. 3) • Not lording (v. 3)

Note: Items in bold occur on all three list, italicized items occur on two of the lists.

Chapter 4

Effective Elder Selection

David Roadcup

One of the critical, beginning steps of building of an effective elder team is using a planned and focused selection process. The decision concerning who should be invited to serve as elder should be bathed in prayer with great care and diligence. In this volume, we have emphasized the critical importance of the role of elders and their leadership. It is a wonderful and weighty responsibility to fulfill the role of elder in the Lord's church. Hebrews 13:17 states, "Obey your leaders and submit to them, for they keep watch over your souls as those who will give an account. Let them do this with joy and not grief, for this would be unprofitable for you." Elders and primary leaders who serve the church effectively will be blessed by God. He will also call each to give an account of their service and ministry to the church.

We need quality elders and elder teams to be trained and to function as effectively as possible when it comes to leading our congregations. As stated previously, *as the leadership of the church goes, so goes the church.* If this is true, then from the beginning, the selection process needs to be done with prayer, careful planning, forethought and serious execution.

In this chapter, we will focus on the functional aspects of elder selection and how it can be done with effectiveness and productivity. It must be pointed out that there are numerous approaches and procedures used in different churches to select elders. In this chapter, we will examine the Scriptural background and include practical observations, especially in helping new congregations find a good plan to select new elders. It will also encourage established congregations to examine their approach to elder selection and will offer ideas to improve and strengthen their present elder selection process.

☎ **Reflection Question:** How would you describe your journey into the eldership? What do you wish had happened better?

Scriptural Directions

In the New Testament, there is a limited amount of information concerning how elder selection should be done. Since the churches of the N.T. were new church plants, it makes sense that the Apostle Paul or one of his co-workers would appoint elders, especially in the churches of South Galatia where there were not large numbers of mature, spiritual leaders present.

There are two references in the New Testament, one by Luke and the other by Paul to point us to this conclusion. Luke gives this report in Acts 14:23, referring to Paul and the churches he had planted. He writes, "When they had appointed elders for them in every church, having prayed with fasting, they commended them to the Lord in whom they had believed." In this instance, Paul had apparently appointed elders himself in the churches he had planted. Paul gives direction to Titus to do the same and asks him to appoint elders in the churches that had been established on the isle of Crete. In Titus:1:5, Paul writes, "For this reason, I left you in Crete, that you would set in order what remains and appoint elders in every city as I directed you."[1]

Therefore, the Biblical pattern simply tells us that Paul and his workers, after planting the churches and working to help the new believers develop and grow, would proceed and appoint those who were to prepared to be elders. Commentator William Ramsey's observation states, "It is clear, therefore, that Paul everywhere instituted elders in his new churches; and on our hypothesis as to the accurate and methodical expression of the historian, we are bound to infer that this first case is intended to be typical of the way of appointment followed in all later cases."[2]

Gene Getz in his excellent book on Eldership writes, "Rather, Paul simply gave Timothy-and us-qualifications, guidelines, and principles, trusting that those of us who read his letters will develop approaches that indeed evaluate whether or not an individual is spiritually qualified to serve."[3]

What we have before us, then, is this; Paul identified qualifications (1 Timothy 3:7; Titus 1: 5-9) which would fit the type of man who would be put forth to be an example and lead the flock. Peter, also (1 Peter 5:1-5) describes the type of man who would be called to fulfill the role of elder and shepherd in a church. Common sense dictates that these men would be Godly, wise, experienced, sensible, dependable, mature men with the mind of Christ. Many of them would be men who have the leadership gift. These men would all "step into the harness together" to protect and lead the church. There are several approaches in our day and time as to how the selection process is executed. Some approaches to the selection of elders may be better than others, but as long as the approach used produces the final result of Godly, spiritual, mature men shepherding the church, it could be considered a functional approach.

Individual Church Dynamics in the Selection Process

In researching various approaches to selecting elders in different congregations, we found that there are numerous ways in which churches do elder selection. Many churches have a directional statement in their by-laws which lays the guidelines for selecting elders. Some churches work mainly through a Selection Team (or Committee) made up of various segments of the congregation's members. Others have decided that having the eldership of the church lead the selection process is preferable. Some churches create a combination of elders, staff and church members to form the Selection Team. Some churches have the congregation submit names of elder candidates. Other churches do not ask congregation members to submit names but request that the Selection Team identify qualified men who desire to serve. In some cases, just the elder team decides on specific men they know and have vetted to approach. The size of the church may also dictate how the church goes about selecting their elder team members. A particular approach may be used in a church that has 120 in attendance, given the nature of their size and relationships. However, a church that averages 2,500 may need to use another method due to their size and large congregational base. There is nothing in Scripture that dictates the details of how this should be done. Churches use various approaches to be sure with the hope that the process used secures the very best men possible to serve and lead.

☎ **Reflection Question:** How has your perception of the eldership changed since joining it?

Different Approaches to Elder Selection

Several different approaches will now be listed as examples of how functioning churches select their elders. Various aspects of some of these approaches may differ from how your particular church presently does elder selection. Some may be very similar. For your examination:

First Christian Church

1. Elders currently serving decide to search for additional elders.
2. The elders draw a list of potential candidates from the active membership role of the Church.

3.   The elders will prayerfully review the list of potential candidates and select those men who will be invited to consider the possibility of serving as an elder.

4. Should the candidate wish to proceed with this process, he is then asked to complete a thorough written questionnaire, which provides a depth of background information regarding the candidate.

5. The elders review each completed questionnaire and further identify likely candidates.

6. In light of the information gathered from the questionnaires and other methods, one or more in-depth interviews will take place with each candidate.

7. The candidates next attend an orientation to learn all that is involved in serving as an elder.

8. Using all of this information, the elders prayerfully reach a final selection of those men who will be recommended to the Church membership for their affirmation.

9. An 8 hour training seminar is conducted for the men who desire to accept this assignment.

9. The elders will make known the names of the candidates to the Church membership and allow a two week time frame for any concerns regarding a candidate to be expressed privately to an elder who is currently serving.

10. Following the affirmation by the Church members, the new elders will officially begin their new ministry with a time of prayer, fasting and dedication in a public worship service.

Northside Church of Christ

1.   The elders assemble a Selection Team who begin meeting on a regular basis. This team is made up of 2 elders, 1 or 2 staff members and 7 members from the congregation, at large.

2.   The congregation is informed that elder nominations are being received for consideration. They will have 30 days to fill out a nomination form provided by the elders and Selection Team for candidates they may wish to nominate.

3.   The Selection Team will prayerfully consider the people nominated. Selection Team members will also have the chance to nominate candidates, as well.

4.   From the pool of candidates, people who have a desire to serve and fulfill the qualifications of Scripture will be approached and invited to be considered as candidate for elder.

5.   The names of those on the final list will then be submitted to the elders for final approval.

6.   Men who are accepted candidates and desire to serve will be contacted by the elders and invited to attend training/informational sessions to communicate to the candidates the ministry, role and expectations of someone serving in the eldership.

7.   In prayer and fasting, the new elders will be formally presented and introduced to the congregation in the worship service(s) of the church, beginning their tenure of service.

Using information gathered from Scripture, experience and research, a suggested plan is presented in this chapter which will produce very good results in a quality elder selection process. If your church is a new church plant, you can adopt this approach in total. If your church has a plan in place that has used for years, why not consider taking pieces of this plan and incorporating them into your present approach to improve and strengthen your present process?

A Suggested Approach to Effective Elder Selection

1. *Announce to the church that the process of elder selection is beginning and call the church to fasting and prayer.*

Since so much in the life of a fruitful church depends on its leaders, the church should be made aware of the seriousness of the fact that elder selection is starting. Bring the church as a whole into this process. Ask for people to participate, not only by nominating possible candidates but by also entering into a time of serious prayer and fasting. Ask people to pray daily for the Lord to lead the right men to the elder team. Why not ask believers to fast through one meal a week the month before and lift this process and its outcome up to the Lord? If your church has not fasted together, this could be an excellent opportunity to teach the church about fasting and its importance in the life of a congregation.

2. Decide on who will form the elder selection team.

Different churches have different approaches when it comes to deciding on the selection of names for new elder possibilities. The church's by-laws should be consulted for clarity and possibly changed if need be to reflect the most effective method of elder selection. If there is nothing in the by-laws, the elders should simply set policy about this administrative point. Some churches have their elders name a Selection Team from various segments of the church. As mentioned, a team like this may have 2 elders, 3 deacons or ministry team leaders and 5-6 laypersons on the team. In other churches, the elders form the selection team. This may especially be true in the case of mega-church elder selection. The large size of the congregation may call for just the elders to make up the selection team. Either of these approaches will work, depending on the circumstances of the church. A team should be selected and a chairperson should be appointed with the team working until the process is complete.

3. Compile an initial list of candidates.

A list of people who desire to serve as elders should be assembled. It is recommended that the congregation be given the chance to suggest names to the selection team. This can be done informally or nomination forms can be provided to the congregation by placing them in the church's bulletins, putting them at the Information Center or providing them through the church's website and having people submit them electronically. The paid staff, present elders, Selection Team and congregation members should submit names. A final date for submission should be set and communicated to the congregation.

4. *The list of names is completed which identify those who meet the Biblical standard and desire to serve.*

Those who are executing the process should compile the list of names from names that have been suggested. The team as a whole  should begin the process of deciding who viable candidates are. Those who are confirmed should be contacted formally and asked their interest level in serving as elder. Those who are definitely interested should continue the process. Those not desiring the position should be excused. Other men, though nominated, may not be ready to serve as elder for a variety of reasons. Those not ready to serve should be personally contacted and informed that they should continue the process of preparation. This part of the process can prove to be a very sensitive issue. It should be handled with care and with a shepherd's heart.

5. *Candidate information and congregational feedback is obtained and analyzed.*

An elder information questionnaire should be distributed to each candidate for completion. This questionnaire should ask for information concerning the candidate's personal and family background, spiritual conversion, relationship to Christ and theological beliefs. In smaller churches, much of this information is known simply by years spent together and length of relationships. In large churches, this information may not be as known or as clear to those doing the evaluating. Therefore, a process involving the filling out of a questionnaire and a face to face evaluation can prove necessary and helpful.

In addition to the personal questionnaire, those doing the evaluating may want to consider the use of a psychological evaluation or personality test as part of the process. The information from an evaluation instrument can be of great help in getting to know the candidate and how he will fit into the existing elder team.[4]

Any feedback or observations from members of the congregation should also be considered and an inquiry should be made concerning the issue(s) of concern.

It is quite possible that the information which comes to the interviewers could reveal issues which would eliminate someone from consideration. If this happens, the candidate should be contacted and an appointment made with him to discuss the situation. This should not be seen necessarily as a negative situation. This could become a good opportunity to share with the candidate concerning the fact that growth is necessary in their walk with Christ prior to their serving as elder. This opportunity and heart-felt discussion could help them grow and ultimately strengthen them in their spiritual journey. These meetings should always be covered in prayer and should be done with love, genuine concern and humility on the part of the interviewers.

6. *Elder candidates are personally interviewed and assessed.*

Each candidate should be personally interviewed after the questionnaire is completed, possible test results are obtained and all information evaluated. The interview should be positive and supportive of the candidate, while still gleaning the necessary information and insight needed to know the candidate, his reputation and background.

7. *Orientation and training session is conducted.*

People who are going to be elders need to be encouraged, supported and trained. This is basic to the functioning and effective work of a qualified and productive elder. In his book titled, *Biblical Leadership*, Alexander Strauch makes this point in an emphatic way as he states, "If you are a pastor or missionary-founder of a church, it is absolutely essential to realize that the elders and potential elders need training. Most newly founded elderships fail because those involved simply do not know enough, or are not skilled enough, to do the work. Without a conscious effort to train elders and share the pastoral oversight with them, biblical eldership will turn into another empty church theory. Training elders is a key part of the transition and implementation of biblical eldership.[5]

Each candidate wanting to serve should be asked to attend orientation and training sessions. The length and content of these sessions greatly vary from church to church. The sessions should cover important and helpful information for the new candidate. Elder training should be comprehensive, covering key topics and areas of important information. A suggested time frame for leadership training should possibly be eight hours or more. An all day Saturday training seminar, Wednesday evenings for a specific period of time or a weekend retreat would all work well. A church in the Atlanta, Georgia area has an approach that calls for men who want to become elders to successfully participate in a ministry that meets each month for a year. This training approach asks the men to attend required meetings, read key materials and participate in two training retreats during the year's period. At the end of this experience, the church knows the candidate well and his training has been extensive for his elder preparation. Several churches researched ask elder candidates to lead groups in their small group ministry as part of their preparation for elder work. This gives the candidate the chance to lead in a smaller setting. The approach to elder training should be determined by the elders and lead staff members. The important thing is that there is an effective elder training ministry in the church that will carefully equip men for the role as servant and leader. There definitely needs to be a concrete plan in place to assure the training and preparation of men preparing to step into the role of elder.

Many elder candidates are not required to experience any formal or significant training whatsoever. The only training some candidates receive is to watch those who have been elders before them and do what they did. While there are benefits to absorbing the power of example, this approach, by itself, is very limited and inadequate when it comes to preparing men to do one of the most significant ministries in the church. Clear principles from Scripture, expectations, role, job description and other topics should be discussed and communicated to elder candidates. Training should cover topics such as:

- God's Call to the Eldership
- The Spiritual Life of the Elder
- Biblical and Practical Qualifications for Elders
- The Biblical Job Description of the Elder
- The Church as an Organism vs. the Church as an Organization
- How Effective Elders Lead
- Expectations and Role of Elder at First Christian Church
- Discovering and Using Your Spiritual Gifts as an Elder
- Building and Maintaining Good Relationships
- The Importance of Hospitality in the Life of an Elder

The training should prepare the elder candidate to understand not only Scriptural guidelines and directives but also the expectations and needs of the congregation where the candidate will serve. Each congregation is different, having developed its own culture over the years. Training should provide the specific information needed by each candidate to do the very best work, possible.

It is a good idea to put key points of agreement and requirements on paper for the elder candidate and church members, alike to consider. A copy of one example of this can be found in Appendix 4.1.

☎ **Reflection Question:** On a scale of ① ② ③ ④ ⑤ ⑥ ⑦, low to high, how well prepared were you to enter the eldership? What could have improved this?

8. *Congregational Confirmation*

If the process used calls for the congregation to confirm by vote the new elder candidates, this should be done at this point by paper ballet. A date is set and announced and the vote takes place in the Sunday service or all weekend services. (If no congregational confirmation is necessary, Step 8 can be eliminated.)

9. *New elders are confirmed, presented to the congregation, and begin their term of service.*

Each elder candidate who has completed the above process is then confirmed to his new position. This should be done in a very visible and celebratory way with the congregation.

At all of the church's weekend worship services (for churches who may have multiple services during the weekend) all confirmed candidates are presented by the elders to the congregation in all services. Many congregations will have a brief elder ordination service. The new elder(s) kneel and experience the laying on of hands by the present elders as a symbol of their being set aside for their new ministry.

☎ **Reflection Question:** If you, as an individual elder, could make one change to the way in which elders are selected, what would it be?

Frequently Asked Questions about Elder Selection

Question: *How about the age factor in elder selection? How young can a man be and still be ordained as an elder?" Can a man be too old to serve as elder?*

Answer – In terms of being young, it is very much of a case by case matter. It is very hard to place a specific age on how young a man can be and still become an elder. Some men can be prepared and very mature on a number of fronts in their late 20s or early 30s. A man at that age may have completed his education, married, had children, is a manager at work or owns his own business. He may be prepared to take the role of elder. Others in this age range or even older may need more time to mature and grow spiritually and in life experience. Some church by-laws may have a statement indicating how young/old a man must be to become an elder, which should be a consideration. In terms of older men, a man can successfully function as an elder as long as he has the desire and is mentally, emotionally, physically and spiritually able. Some men are promoted to Elder Emeritus after a long period of fruitful service.

Question – *"Can a person have been divorced in his past and still be ordained an elder?"*

Answer – In Paul's list of Biblical qualifications in I Timothy, he states that a man should be a "one womaned man" (literal translation). Paul is giving instruction here that an elder should be the husband of only one wife. Does Paul mean by this statement that a man who has a divorce in his past, no matter how long ago or for what reason, be eliminated from serving as an elder for the rest of his life? This was truly not his intent. A man does need to demonstrate his ability to enter into and cultivate his marriage in such a way that longevity is a part of his relationship to his wife. This is the obvious Biblical standard and desired application of Paul's admonition.

There are, however, extenuating circumstances which should be considered.

If an elder's wife commits adultery, Jesus told us that a man is allowed to divorce his wife. In the case of an elder experiencing this situation, he should be supported by the church and his brother elders. It may be advantageous to the elder, himself and to the church to step down from the eldership for a time. Pragmatically, he may resign the rest of his tenure or take a "leave of absence" due to the personal stress and devastation which always follows the breakup of a marriage. Wisdom would tell us that a break in the leadership tenure of this man would be beneficial.

If a man is newly divorced and adultery is not part of the breakup, it is definitely best for the brother to step down from the eldership and let time pass and healing take place. If the man involved as elder desires to regain his position, a lengthy period of time should pass to allow for healing and restoration. This does not mean that the man can never serve as elder again, but there must be a rebuilding of his credibility over the years to allow him to be a part of the leadership of the church.

Tom, who lived in the mid-west, married right out of high school. He and his wife divorced after 6 months. This man graduated from college, took a responsible position in the banking industry, remarried and had two children. In his mid 30s, he found Christ as his savior. He went on to grow in his new found faith and became a

66

very positive influence in his congregation. He came to a place of maturity where he felt he could make a major contribution to the church by serving as an elder. He was denied the opportunity to serve as an elder due to the fact that he had a divorce in his past. The facts that he had found Christ and had become a "new creation" were  not taken into consideration. There are strong and differing opinions on this issue in various churches. It does not appear that Paul would bar this man from exercising his leadership gift because, years ago, before he became a believer, he had struggled with divorce. How has a divorced man handled his life, work, reputation relationships, etc since a divorce 5,8, 10 or 20 years ago? The fact that a mistake was made was obvious but people do learn and grow and change. If a brother has demonstrated over the years that he has learned, grown and has built into his life the teachings of Christ on a much higher plane, he should be given a chance to serve on the church's elder team.

Question – *"Does a man have to be married to become an elder?"*

Answer - A man does not have to be married to be an elder. Single men can serve in the eldership with effectiveness. Paul is indicating that if a man is married, his marriage should reflect dignity and commitment.

Question – *"Does a man have to have children to be an elder?"*

Answer - A man does not have to have children to be an elder. Single men or married men with no children can be very effective elders. Paul gives specific guidelines to married men who do have children who are being considered for the elder position.

Question – *"Can women be ordained as elders?"*

Answer – With entire books being written on this topic, it is impossible to exhaust this issue in this chapter. To get specifically to the main point - there is no question that women provide a vast amount of influence and leadership in the life of the church today. Take the influence, work and leadership of women out of the average church today and most churches would collapse.

The point is very clear in Scripture. In the early church, women taught, preached, led and exerted great influence as the church grew. Scriptures to examine include Acts 2:17 where Peter quotes the prophet Joel who wrote concerning the day of Pentecost and said, "Your sons and daughters will prophecy....". Paul writes of women prophesying in the Corinthian church when in I Cor. 11:5, he says, "But every woman who has her head uncovered while praying or prophesying disgraces her head . . .". Luke tells us that Phillip had four daughters who prophesied (Acts 21:9). As to whether women preached, taught, organized and administered ministries in the early church, there is no question. It should be the same today. Women should be able to do everything that a man can do (lead a ministry team, direct a choir or worship, deliver a sermon or exhortation, organize, administer, and evangelize). Women are greatly valued and prized in the Lord's eyes.

There is one limitation that Paul makes in I Timothy 2. He discusses the issue of a woman exercising authority over a man. He indicates the theological point of Eve's sin as precedence for women not usurping authority over men. This issue is not just dealing with cultural norms. Paul sites the order of creation and Eve's sin as issues in making his point. So, with great respect and admiration for women in the church and their immense contribution to the life of the church and the building of the kingdom, we must deduce from the Scriptures that women can do everything men can do in the church with the exception of usurping authority over men. This then does preclude then that women should not be placed on the eldership of the church.

Question – *"When elders are ordained, does that mean that they are elders for the rest of their lives?"*

Answer - Scripture is silent on this issue. There are no specific directives from Paul or any other Biblical author on this issue. It would appear that the ministry of being an elder has a specific purpose, that being among other assignments, to shepherd the flock. As long as a man is fulfilling that role, he could be considered an elder (formally or informally). When he ceases leading in that specific function or cannot lead because of extenuating circumstances, it may be that he no longer is fulfilling the role of elder and should not be considered an elder, formally.

☎ **Group Reflection Questions**

- How involved is your congregation in the process of elder selection?
- Can you think of any ways in which they could be involved at a greater level?
- How well explained is the process of elder selection in your congregation?
- Can you tangibly identify an intentional process of training elders for your congregation? If yes, what is it? If not, why not?

Endnotes

[1]For thorough discussions of Biblical passages and words dealing with these two passages and other content, refer to Gene A. Getz, *Elders and Leaders* (Chicago: Moody Press, 2003), pp.201-208 and Alexander Strauch, *Biblical Eldership* (Lewis and Roth, 1995), pp. 101-120.

[2]William Ramsey, *St. Paul the Traveler and the Roman Citizen*, 3rd edition (Grand Rapids: Baker Book House, 1951), p. 121.

[3]Getz, *Elders and Leaders*, p. 208.

[4] Possible Psychological or Personality Inventories or Testing Instruments might include the DiSC Personal Profile System 2800 Series C-128, The Myers-Briggs Type Indicator or The Taylor-Johnson Temperament Analysis test.

[5]Strauch, Biblical Eldership, p. 284.

Appendix 4.1

Heritage Leadership Commitment

Knowing that God has spoken clearly through His Word concerning the character and responsibility of His church leaders, I do seriously commit myself to God, the leadership, and the community of our church to the following:

1. I agree with the Statement of Faith of Heritage Christian Church without reservation.

2. I will maintain a close and intimate walk with the Lord by spending time on a regular basis alone with Him in prayer and as a diligent student of His Word. As a part of that prayer time, I will pray for our church, our staff and other leaders in the life of our church and will pray that God alone will receive the glory in all the ministries of the church.

3. As a godly example and role model to all people, I will be above reproach in all matters regarding my personal, professional, spiritual and social life. I will carefully manage my habits, attitudes and witness as a servant of Christ to those within our church and to those without, always striving to glorify the Lord through my example in conduct, faith and love.

4. I am in agreement with the philosophy and direction of Heritage Christian Church in using contemporary methods in music, worship, outreach, missions and shepherding.
5. I will consider my family as my most important earthly gift from God, will manage it well and model servant leadership in my home.
6. I have fulfilled the one-year Elder/Leadership Training or Mentoring Experience here at HCC.
7. I commit to make my leadership and service to our church a major priority in my life in terms of time commitment. I commit to attend leadership meetings and church functions with dependability and earnestness, serving with a positive attitude and Christ-like spirit.
8. I commit to manage my finances carefully, pledging to be a consequential giver in the life of our church. I will commit at least 10% of my income to the Lord's work. Additionally, I will give the first 10% to God through Heritage Christian Church as an example of my commitment to the ministry of the local church body I serve.
9. By the power of the Holy Spirit, I will refrain from negative attitudes through criticism and complaint. Instead, I will be positive and encouraging to all, endeavoring to maintain the unity of the Spirit in the bond of peace.
10. I will maintain an open and teachable attitude.

I have studied and prayed over these statements of commitment and believe that God, through the power of the Holy Spirit, would have me serve as an Elder of H.C.C.

Signed _____ Date _____

Chapter 5

Elder Governance

Gary L. Johnson

**"Opportunity is missed by most people because
it is dressed in overalls and looks like work."**
Thomas Edison

While driving to and from work or across the country on vacation, there is a sad reality marking the American landscape—closed churches. Regretfully, thousands of churches are estimated to close up shop this year and every year. If not purchased by or given to another church group, a closed church may be used for a variety of purposes. Some churches have been remodeled into homes, and even into condominiums. Some churches have morphed into businesses, such as becoming an antique shop. Closed churches serve as a sad commentary on life in the American culture. While clinging to traditions and methods of the past, the local church fails to focus on the present and future. Leadership fails to develop new methods and paradigms of "doing church." As a result, the church continues to decline both spiritually and numerically, and before long, the church is closed—only to become an antique shop, where rusty relics of the past are sought and bought.

Still, an exciting opportunity lies before us, but it is dressed in overalls and looks like hard work. That opportunity is to let go of past traditions used in structuring the local church, and work to develop new, internal structures that actually promote potential numerical growth within the church. Making such changes is hard work.

God created the human body to grow. An essential part of the human body is the skeletal system. Without our skeletons, we could not physically grow or function. From even within the womb, the human body begins to grow. God designed our bones to grow in length, width and density so that the human body can increase in size. The skeleton has primary functions. For example, the skeleton provides the human body with shape and support, while the skeletal joints enable the body to move. Further, the skeleton produces life-giving blood components, while storing necessary nutrients such as calcium. Without the human skeleton—our internal structure—it would be impossible for our bodies to grow and function effectively.

In the same manner, God designed the Church to grow numerically as more people become followers of Jesus Christ. After all, God wants no man to perish, but to come to repentance (2 Peter 3:9). For the church to grow, it is essential to have an effective internal structure that accommodates growth. Christian Schwarz, in *Natural Church Development*, cites having functional structures as a necessary component of church growth. Having completed extensive research of over one thousand churches in thirty two countries on six continents, Schwarz has observed, "Wherever God breathes His Spirit into formless clay, both life and form spring forth."[1]

There is a pressing need for the Church to look analytically at the internal structure of the organization. This structure is called polity, a particular form or system of governing the church. How a local church is internally structured has much to do with the effectiveness of ministry, particularly reaching people who are not yet believers, and transforming them into fully devoted followers of Jesus Christ. The Church is a living, spiritual entity, one described by the Apostle Paul as being like that of a human body with many parts (1 Corinthians 12:12-27), and an essential element of the body of Christ is the internal structure, or polity.

☎ **Reflection Question:** What words would you use to describe the internal structure of your church?

The First Century Church

In Acts 6:1-7, the first century church models for us the importance of internal structures. Faced with a crisis, the early church did not ignore an internal issue that could have caused division within the ranks. Instead, the leaders addressed the issue effectively.

Verse 1

"In those days when the number of disciples was increasing, the Grecian Jews among them complained against the Hebraic Jews because their widows were being overlooked in the daily distribution of food."

"In those days" refers to the early church in her earliest beginnings. This could have been in the first few months, or even the first few years, when the number of disciples (i.e., followers of the Way) kept growing numerically. The word for "increasing" is in present tense, meaning that the numerical growth continued and did not cease.

The growing numbers of believers resulted in some growing pains: Greek-speaking widows were being neglected when food was distributed to those in need. The Hebrew-speaking widows were getting food, but not Greek-speaking widows, and this did not happen only once or twice, but repeatedly as an imperfect tense in Greek is used for the word "overlook".

Why there were so many Greek-speaking widows in Jerusalem? Simply answered, they wanted to be there. On the Day of Pentecost, tens of thousands of Jewish people were in Jerusalem for the Feast of Pentecost. Acts 2 indicates that when the Holy Spirit was given and the Church was created, three thousand Jewish people came to believe that Jesus was the Messiah. Many of those Jews came from countries in which Greek was spoken as the primary language. Some of those people stayed in Jerusalem after Pentecost, enjoying the sense of community described in Acts 2:42-47. Life was exciting, and the Church was a dynamic group of people doing life at deep levels of satisfaction, and Greek-speaking widows would have been within that group. Moreover, Hellenistic Jews often moved to Jerusalem in their old age, wanting to live out their final days in the Holy City. When the women out-lived their husbands, there were no grown children to care for them in the area.

Verses 2-4

"So the Twelve gathered all the disciples together and said, "It would not be right for us to neglect the ministry of the word of God in order to wait on tables. Brothers, choose seven men from among you who are known to be full of the Spirit and wisdom. We will turn this responsibility over to them and will give our attention to prayer and the ministry of the word."

The apostles proposed a significant change to their internal structure. They knew they had to do something because the complaining was just a symptom of a greater problem, that being prejudice. Two ethnic groups were clashing and if ignored, the

 church could suffer great harm. The leaders did not point a finger of blame at anyone except themselves. They knew they were being stretched too thin, and they were unable to be faithful to their primary calling, that being prayer and the ministry of the Word (i.e., "ministry" is *diakonia* meaning "to labor"). They wanted to labor at prayer and making known the Word of God. This situation accentuates their need for internal structure to accommodate the ministry demands of a large, continually growing church.

Not ignoring this need, the apostles created a polity (internal structure) that would meet the needs of those being overlooked. The apostles wanted to effectively delegate responsibility to another leadership level. The first century church was very Jewish in practice, as seen in this situation. This distribution of food was called the custom of the *kuppah* (i.e., basket). Individuals went from house to house to collect food and money for those in need, particularly for widows and orphans who had no family to care for their needs. This collection was made with a *kuppah,* or basket. So, to continue this benevolent ministry in a rapidly growing church required a more effective internal structure.

Verses 5-6

> *"This proposal pleased the whole group. They chose Stephen, a man full of faith and of the Holy Spirit; also Philip, Procorus, Nicanor, Timon, Parmenas, and Nicolas from Antioch, a convert to Judaism. They presented these men to the apostles, who prayed and laid their hands on them."*

When they implemented the new structural method of feeding all the widows, it was immediately embraced by the believers. The leaders even solved the problem with people who were a part of the group impacted by the problem: Greeks. The Greek-speaking widows would be certain to receive food because the seven men chosen to lead and serve at this new level all had Greek names. The seven men were presented to the apostles, who then prayed and laid hands on them, which was a visible symbol of communicating that both responsibility and authority had been given to them.

Verse 7

> *"So the word of God spread. The number of disciples in Jerusalem increased rapidly, and a large number of priests became obedient to the faith."*

There is a particular Greek tense in this verse that is used three times, and the tense means that the action referred to continued without ceasing. The Word of God kept spreading, and then spread some more. This does not mean that more and more books of the Bible were being written, but that the Word of God kept spreading into the lives of people, having life-changing impact. Moreover, the number of new disciples kept increasing. More Jewish priests became obedient to the Christian faith as they also converted. Christianity made enormous inroads within the Jewish leadership in Jerusalem. The first century Jewish historian Josephus wrote that there were four tribes of priests, each with roughly 5,000 priests, making for roughly 20,000 Jewish priests in Jerusalem and a large number of them became obedient to the Christian faith.[2] Why? Leaders were willing to change internal structures within the first century church.   The church remained unified, while the church multiplied.

The Twenty-First Century Church

Just as leaders intentionally changed the traditional internal structure of the first century church, leaders in the twenty-first century church must be willing to do the same—if we hope to create an environment that fosters continual growth in the number of people coming to faith in Christ. Have you noticed anything different when opening a bottle of Bayer aspirin? The Bayer Corporation has stopped putting cotton wads in their Genuine Bayer aspirin bottles. The company discovered that the aspirin would be preserved without the thick, plump white cotton wads that had been inserted since 1914. Leaders at Bayer admitted that there was no viable reason to keep using the cotton other than to maintain a tradition. Once they made this decision to break with tradition, consumers were benefitted in that they could more easily use the aspirin because the cotton was difficult to remove. Bayer made a good decision that reflected well on their purpose of existence.

The Church exists to pick up where Jesus left off. Jesus said that He had been "sent into the world to seek and to save what was lost" (Luke 19:10), and in turn, He said to His disciples, "As the Father has sent Me, so I am sending you" (John 20:21). We have been sent by Jesus to seek the lost. We are to make disciples of all people groups

(Matthew 28:18-20). In order to accomplish our mission, an effective internal structure is essential.

Far too many congregations have a polity in place that is restrictive in nature. Church boards have a tendency to micromanage people, making it necessary for individuals to "jump through hoops" of regulations and by-laws. Church leadership teams that make motions and vote following Roberts Rules of Order create a divisive environment where some people win and some people lose depending on the outcome of the vote. Such board behavior and practices always divide people. A church board mentality keeps a church from growing. In contrast, a church that develops and implements an internal structure of elder governance will create an evangelistic environment, fostering continual numerical growth. To understand elder governance, we must first understand a recent movement called policy governance.

☎ **Reflection Question:** How much time each week do you actually spend working on church-related tasks?

The History of Policy Governance

Dr. John Carver (www.policygovernance.com) is the internationally recognized creator of the policy governance model, now being implemented by governing boards around the world. Policy governance is a results-oriented approach to board operations, making leadership more effective in how they lead an organization. Policy governance understands that "the board is at the top of any organization, with authority and accountability for that organization."[3]

Policy governance is a theory or approach to board operations, and can be implemented by organizations at will. Policy governance is based on fundamental principles, such as trust, as those who lead organizations are answerable to their constituents. As well, a board speaks with one voice, which helps to create a spirit of unanimity. A board, which operates under policy governance, makes policy decisions that are a reflection of the values and vision of the board. Once policies are in place, the board delegates responsibility and authority to the principle leader of the organization (i.e., the CEO, etc.) to lead the staff.

In the Carver model of Board Governance, "ends" (i.e., outcomes) are the focus of those on the governing board, while "means" (i.e., methods for accomplishing the outcomes) are the focus of the organization's staff. Churches that have adopted the Carver Policy Governance model for their internal structure must exercise caution in that elders do not focus strictly on outcomes or "ends," but that they remain participatory in the "means" or methods of accomplishing the outcomes for the congregation. A blended, or hybrid, form of governance can be developed, known as elder governance.

Elder Governance

In much the same manner, elder governance is a theory or approach to leading the local congregation, making the internal structure of the church more effective. When the polity of the local church is more effective, there is potential for the church to be healthier, and a healthy church is a growing church.

Elder governance embraces similar principles of policy governance. For example, there is the principle of trust. The Apostle Paul wrote, "Now it is required that those who have been given a trust must prove faithful" (1 Corinthians 4:2). Elders—and others at a higher level of leadership in the local church—have been given a trust by God, and they must be faithful in that responsibility. As well, Jesus taught a parable of the ten talents (see Matthew 25:14-30), in which His Kingdom has been entrusted to leaders. These leaders will be held accountable by Jesus at His second coming for how they led His Church in His absence.

Elder governance calls for unanimity among elders, which is then expressed in "one voice." Unity is of vital importance to Jesus, as He prayed that we would be one as He and the Father are one, and that we would be brought to complete unity (John 17:20-23). On the last night of His life, the Church was the focus of the prayers of Jesus, which calls Christ-followers to strive for unity, particularly among those who have been entrusted with His Church.

Elder governance makes policy decisions. Rather than micro-manage church staff and volunteers, elders using this policy establish policies to be followed by others within the local church. Once policies are established and implemented, elders are able to focus on issues that are more spiritual in nature.

Elder governance intentionally delegates responsibility and authority to others, particularly in the area of their spiritual gifting and calling. Only by establishing policies can elders effectively delegate responsibilities to people, accompanied with the authority to exercise ministry.

When a congregation is organized according to elder governance, there are four primary functions of an elder team. To stay focused on these four primary tasks, the elders can arrange a meeting agenda using these four categories, and if an issue does not fit into one of these categories, it is likely that the task should be handled by another leadership team within the church.

The four primary functions within elder governance are: 1) to establish policy, 2) to lead the ministry of prayer, 3) to lead the ministry of the Word, and 4) provide oversight in pastoral matters. Day-to-day operational matters are not the concern of elders, nor are administrative or financial issues. These responsibilities—and their accompanying authority by which to get the job done—are to be delegated by the elders to individuals capable of leading in those areas.

☎ **Reflection Question:** Can your internal structure—polity—be improved? If so, how?

A Description of an Elder's Four Functions

First, Elder governance calls for establishing policy. In Acts 15, the apostles and elders in Jerusalem established a policy regarding outreach to Gentiles. There was a significant dispute in the early church, which resulted in what is referred to as the Jerusalem Council. A dispute arose in the church at Antioch, making it necessary for Paul, Barnabas and Peter to settle this matter with church leaders. The issue was over whether a Gentile had to be circumcised in order to be saved. James, who has been called the "chief elder" of the Jerusalem church, rendered a "policy decision" beginning in verse 13 ("listen to me"). The elders sent Paul and Barnabas back to Antioch with instructions not to make it too difficult for the Gentiles, who were turning to God. A policy was established and issued. Moreover, both responsibility and authority were given to church leaders to do ministry according to the policy. Paul, Barnabas and others were not micro-managed as they carried out their ministry. Therefore, elder governance refuses to micro-manage church staff. Elders establish policies for the church. The staff will be highly involved in the writing of policy drafts, which are then reviewed, edited (if needed), and adopted by the elders. Elders oversee the compiling of a written Policy Manual. Policies provide parameters for the operation of the church. Elders delegate the authority to the staff to operate the church (i.e., decision making). This environment is referred to as being "staff led—elder protected."

Second, Elder governance calls for oversight of pastoral matters. The above text (Acts 15:1f, the Jerusalem Council) also highlights the pastoral nature of the elders' ministry. In verse 4, Paul and his companions "reported in" (i.e., they were being held accountable) to James, the Just, and the other elders of the church in Jerusalem. The elders in Jerusalem had sent Barnabas to Antioch to do ministry among the Gentiles. Both Paul and Barnabas had a sense of accountability to the elders in Jerusalem.

The very nature of this matter was highly spiritual in content, and so it was deferred to the elders as a matter of pastoral concern. Therefore, elders are involved in the lives of people within the congregation, in particular, by establishing a culture of accountability with one another. Elders "send out" those who have prepared for full time Christian ministry, and an accountable relationship is established between these individuals and the elders. People are ordained by the local church only after successfully completing both written and oral exams administered by the elders to determine an individual's capability to represent the gospel of Jesus Christ as an ordained minister. Those "sent out" from the local church are provided pastoral care and continuing ministry development in a covenant relationship with the ordaining church.

In Acts 20:28, the Apostle Paul urged the elders in the church at Ephesus to "be shepherds" of the church. Elders are involved in providing pastoral care in the area of spiritual matters, which includes, but is not limited to caring for emotional, spiritual and physical needs of people, caring for relational needs of people, as well as administering church discipline when deemed necessary. Elders minister pastorally to people who are ill, shut-in, spiritually in-active, grieving, etc. To that end, elders are visibly present in the lives of people, whether that is in the church, in their homes, at hospitals, etc.

Third, Elder governance calls for the ministry of prayer. In Acts 6:1-7, the apostles emphasized their need to minister to people through prayer. By appointing the first deacons to oversee the physical needs of widows in need of food, the spiritual leaders in the early church devoted themselves to prayer. By delegating operational tasks to others, elders in the 21ˢᵗ century church can devote themselves to the ministry of prayer. Therefore, elders are intentionally—and persistently—involved in prayer. Elders make themselves more readily and visibly available for intercessory prayer, particularly during corporate worship. Elders must develop a reputation among the believers as being powerful in prayer (James 5:16). Elders lead in prayer by example (1 Corinthians 11:1). We cannot expect people in the local church to develop powerful prayer lives if the spiritual leaders of the church are not modeling the same behavior.

Finally, Elder governance calls for the ministry of the Word. In Acts 20, the Apostle Paul said farewell to the elders of the church in Ephesus. It is interesting to note that he prophesied that from these men, some elders would arise and distort the truth (verse 30). After he left Ephesus, Timothy became the minister of that congregation, and Paul found it necessary to write to Timothy and tell him to "stay in Ephesus to command certain men not to teach false doctrine" (1 Timothy 1:3). Who were these men? They were from among the elders of the church! In his farewell to the Ephesian elders, Paul commanded them to "guard the flock that is under their care." Hence, elders are to guard the doctrinal purity of the Church through the ministry of the Word. Therefore, elders protect believers from false doctrine. Elders must have significant scriptural knowledge in order to guard the doctrinal purity of the church (i.e., what is taught, preached, believed, etc.). Elders must foster an environment of continual learning, modeling biblical literacy for the congregation. Elders must live the Word, as well as know the Word.

☎ **Reflection Question:** What is your level of involvement in the typical elder's meeting? How would you describe a typical elders' meeting where you serve?

Years ago, people enjoyed watching the ever-popular television show *The Wide World of Sports*. During the opening few moments of each episode, the viewer saw a downhill skier attempting a ski jump, a visual way of understand this show's familiar mantra, "the thrill of victory and the agony of defeat." As the athlete began his descent, all appeared to be going well. But, for no apparent reason, the skier wiped out, and plummeted into the side of the ski run. What most viewers did not know was that the athlete chose this radical change of direction. He chose to fall. Why? The surface of the ski run had become too icy, and he knew that would likely land far past the safe landing area, endangering his life and those of spectators. Making this change was painful, but it could have been fatal had he not made the change.

☎ **Reflection Question:** How open is your leadership to change? Be specific.

Changing the internal structure of the local church can be hard, painful work. If we choose to make this change, we can experience the "thrill of victory" as more people can be brought to Christ, as in the first century church. Yet, failing to make this painful change, can result in the "agony of defeat."

☎ **Group Reflection Questions**
- How did the elders describe the internal structure of your church?
- To what degree are the elders involved in the daily operations of your church?

- What are some ways we could improve the effectiveness and efficiency of elder's meetings?
- As an eldership, what are three obvious improvements that could be made to the congregation's internal organizational structure?
- What arguments typically surface when change is proposed in an elder's meeting? Are these objections legitimate?

Endnotes

[1] Christian A. Schwarz, *Natural Church Development: A Guide to Eight Essential Qualities of Healthy Churches* (St. Charles, IL: ChurchSmart Resources, 2003), p. 28.

[2] Simon J. Kistemaker, *Acts* (Grand Rapids, MI: Baker Book House, 1990), p. 225.

[3] John Carver and Miriam Carver, *Reinventing Your Board: A Step-by-Step Guide to Implementing Policy Governance* (San Francisco, CA: John Wiley & Sons, Inc., 2006), p. 3.

Chapter 6

Peer Evaluations[1]

James Riley Estep, Jr.

No one likes going for a check-up. Doctors listening, prodding, poking, gagging, shining lights, taking x-rays, needles, and perhaps worst of all the familiar snap of a plastic glove on the doctor's hand. If any of this were done *outside* a doctor's office, they'd be arrested for assault! We may not like it, but check-ups are necessary. Without them, we wait until something does go wrong, and by then, it may be too late.

Only two things could make it worse. What if the doctor were a stranger, someone who didn't know you and that you didn't know? You would just be a patient, a folder handed to him by a nurse; a person, but not an individual. More so, what if the doctor were nothing more than a diagnostician? "Well Mr. Smith, you're right, you are running a fever and are sick. Thanks for coming in. Next!" You don't go to a doctor to be diagnosed, you go to be cured, to be restored to health.

This is why *peer evaluations* are actually beneficial. We may not like the idea of having to be evaluated, but just like check-ups, they  are beneficial in the long term. Because they are done by peers, not strangers, it is a time of mutual encouragement and accountability to one another. Since the purpose of these evaluations is not punitive, it is not an occasion to simply identify one another's errors and engage in finger pointing, but rather to honestly assess strengths and weaknesses, with support for improving one's service to the congregation and Kingdom. From this perspective, the purpose of peer evaluation is improvement, it is pastoral, not punitive. In addition, it is a formal process that is done in the community of brother elders.

How do peers assess my service? Peer review is a common form of evaluation, particularly in professional settings. Similarly, if assessment is to be a communal activity, it assumes the involvement of the whole community, not simply one's self and his/her institutional superiors. Peers provide a valuable voice in evaluation because they are *peers*. Who better to evaluate an individual than another individual sharing a similar commitment and conviction within the institution? A fellow elder can empathize, provide insight into life, family, encourage spiritual formation, give advice in conflict situations, explain shepherding ideas, and even teaching resources and tips. Congregations that ask elders to engage in peer evaluation create a cycle of continual improvement within its leadership.

Objections to Peer Evaluation

"Peer evaluation . . . isn't that judging our brother elders? Isn't Jesus against judging one another?" This is a common objection to any form of evaluation in the church, and in particular with its leadership or other volunteers. Actually Jesus did say, "Do not judge, or you too will be judged" (Matthew 7:1). From this one verse many Christian leaders feel justified in *not* performing peer evaluations! However, Jesus is actually voicing his concern over the *unfair* and *unilateral* critical attitude of the Pharisees toward their followers. In the very next verse, Jesus says, "For in the same way you judge others, you will be judged, and with the measure you use, it will be measured to you" (Matthew 7:2). In another instance, he even commends the disciples for reaching a correct judgment in deciding a character issue between two individuals in a parable (Luke 7:43). It is the judgmental attitude of the Pharisees that Jesus questions, not the notion of assessing someone's performance. We also have the admonition of the Apostle Paul to judge even the character of those in the church.

"What business is it of mine to judge those outside the church? Are you not to judge those inside?" (1 Corinthians 5:12). Similarly, assessment is implicit in the establishing of criteria for Christian leaders (e.g. 1 Timothy 3:1-13, Titus 1:5-9, 1 Peter 5:1-4), which requires someone to determine whether individuals will meet the selection criteria while others will not; requiring some form of assessment process to determine qualified elder candidates. Elders must know how to give evaluation without being judgmental, and how to provide beneficial critique, not simply negative criticism.

☎ **Reflection Question:** What are the greatest hindrances to starting peer evaluation among elders?

Value of Peer Evaluation

Michael Woodruff notes that failing to evaluate the performance of any church worker is "the high price of being too nice."[2] What if elders are simply not evaluated? Well, let's apply that notion to other aspects of life. What if you never asked your teenager about school? What if you never reconciled your checkbook with the bank statement? What if you never spent time reflecting on your own life, looking toward your career's future or even retirement? What if you never scheduled a check-up or asked about that strange pain in your chest? Matters left unattended tend to give rise to problems that require attention; problems that could have been avoided or addressed if they had been caught earlier.

Peer evaluation within the eldership has several advantages not only to the elders, but to the congregation as well. *First, "As iron sharpens iron, so one man sharpens another"* (Proverbs 27:17). Peer evaluation is part of the process of forming a band of brothers, elders-helping-elders improve their ministry within the congregation. Church leadership requires the *sharpest* minds, hearts, and hands in the congregation, and this requires continual attention to develop such leaders.

Second, it can promote the formation of relational accountability among congregation leaders. The eldership is a community within the community of faith. As leaders, they are not only accountable to God, to one another. A sense of accountability shared among these men produces personal, spiritual, and pastoral relationship bonds between them. If our fellow elders do not hold us accountable, who will? There is no hierarchy, association, or authority (other than God) who will step in to hold us accountable. We need one another for support and assessment to improve our leadership posture.

Third, regularly scheduled peer evaluation makes them part of the leadership DNA. Truth be told, elders always do evaluation. The problem is they typically wait until a situation erupts that requires it! Without regularly scheduled evaluations, they become episodic. An episode occurs, requiring elders to intervene, and then evaluation happens under the proverbial gun, on the context of a possible conflict situation. When they are regularly scheduled, elders simply know it is time for the annual evaluation and are not necessarily defensive.

Fourth, peer evaluations promote teamwork. "Though one may be overpowered, two can defend themselves. A cord of three strands is not quickly broken" (Ecclesiastes 4:12). Evaluations are an occasion to combine the cords of leadership. The synergy of teamwork is promoted by engaging in evaluation of one another, in a spirit of friendship and service to the cause of Christ and His church.

How do Elders evaluate Each other?

"Remember the central purpose of evaluation – improvement."[3] Peer evaluation is not done with an attitude of superiority, but one of self-improvement and collaborative development as servant leaders within the community of faith. For any system of peer evaluation to be effective, it must have four elements. *First, produce a list of stated expectations for the eldership.* We all have expectations. However, what if each elder has a different list or level of expectation? Without a standardized list of expectations for serving as an elder, a joint understanding on what it means to serve as an elder within the congregation, then evaluation is almost impossible. Elders should first engage in a dialog about expectations, seek insight from congregation members, former elders, pastoral literature, or perhaps even elders from other congregations could provide valuable insight. Once the list has been developed and approved through whatever approval process may be required, the eldership now has a common ruler to measure one another's service as an elder.

☎ **Reflection Question:** Do you as an elder have common expectations for men serving as elders? What are they?

Second, regularly schedule time for peer evaluation, making it part of the leadership DNA. As previously stated, occasional or episodic evaluations are usually too infrequent or irregular to really benefit the elders or congregation. When peer evaluations are made an annual event, regularly scheduled into the calendar and agenda of the eldership, it removes the anxiety that can be associated with it. For example, as a child, sitting in school, when you heard your name read over the PA system, asking you to come to principal's office . . . "What have I done? What's wrong?" When you are sitting at home and your doctor calls for no apparent reason, "Why is he calling? What do I have?" If a meeting isn't regularly scheduled, it produces some degree of anxiety. When it is regularly scheduled, much of the anxiety is diminished, and one can readily prepare for the evaluation.

"Each one should test his own actions. Then he can take pride in himself, without comparing himself to somebody else, for each one should carry his own load" (Galatians 6:4). Peer review is only effective if it is preceded by a period of self evaluation. This can only occur if an elder know that a peer evaluations is scheduled, which means peer evaluations have to be regularly scheduled.

☎ **Reflection Question:** In what ways do we give one another feedback on a consistent and regular basis? If not, why?

Third, actually perform the peer evaluation. Depending on the size of the eldership, it may be done in several ways. It could be done between accountability partners, one-on-one or perhaps in a small group of three or four elders. If an eldership is relatively small in number, it may be elders evaluating an elder. In any case, given that elders have agreed on a common standard and established a routine period of evaluation, it is now a matter of sitting down with one another and discussing how one compares to the expectations. As previously noted, if peer evaluation is preceded by a period of self evaluation, an elder may recognize a weakness or are for concern even prior to it being identified by his peers. If he is given the opportunity to share the results of his self evaluation at the beginning of his peer evaluation session, the elder may share insights about himself that others were going to point out. He may prove to be quite aware of his strengths and weaknesses, allowing his peers to simply affirm his insights and provide encouragement and resource for improvement. In addition, self evaluation may surface items about which one's peers are simply ignorant.

Finally, give the appropriate feedback to the elder. Feedback takes two forms in peer evaluation. Initial feedback will be given during the peer evaluation session. This is inevitable as peers discuss their insights on one another's life, relationships, and performance as leaders within the congregation. The very definition of "peer" assumes that part of the feedback will be in the context of discussion and dialog between one another. A second form of feedback is more formal. The results of the discussion should be summarized into written form, perhaps no more than a page of annotated outline of the elder's self-evaluation and the elders' peer evaluation, noting in particular how the elders will respond to the needs of their fellow elder. This summation can then be shared with the elder for his review and follow-up on any additional questions it may raise.

When these four steps are used as a system of peer evaluation, elders can "offer acute and honest evaluation" as part as part of serving the congregation as a leader.[4]

Resources for Peer Evaluation

What kind of questions do we ask? What tools can we use to conduct peer evaluations? Appendix 6.1 and 6.2 contain two different possible assessment tools. Appendix 6.1 contains a *qualitative* tool, one that assesses an elder by interviewing and discussion, and is hence more holistic. Elders are assessed by *verbal* responses provided about their lives and service. The next appendix, 6.2, contains a *quantitative* tool, one that assesses an elder with a familiar formatted instrument. With this instrument, elders are assessed by numerical responses to various questions, typically used to assess the performance of an elder. In both sample tools, some adjustment to their contents may be required to custom fit them to your congregation. On a final note, no single assessment tool or opinion is enough. Alone they are all inadequate. However, when an individual uses a given tool to assess their own performance, and then those who serve alongside with him use the same or similar tool to provide feedback, a more complete portrait of the elder's performance is given. Hence, evaluation is not just someone looking in a mirror, but having others provide insight and encouragement.

Conclusion

"Never be lacking in zeal, but keep your fervor, serving the Lord" (Romans 12:11). Healthy elderships practice peer review on a regular basis as part of their leadership. When peer evaluations are done in an atmosphere of pastoral concern and personal growth it affirms the Christian values of worth of the individual, commitment to community, and respectful relationship between Christians.

☎ **Reflection Question:** What are the first three steps you can take toward developing a system of peer evaluation among the eldership?

①

②

③

Appendix 6.1

The following is our Elder Evaluation Form from Indian Creek Christian Church (Indianapolis, Indiana) that is completed <u>annually</u> by each elder and then reviewed in a meeting by all of the elders. Our elders do "peer evaluations" in order to hold each other <u>mutually accountable</u> in serving with a standard of excellence.

Name: _____   **Year of Service:** _____

ELDER ACCOUNTABILITY WORKSHEET

"As iron sharpens iron, so one man sharpens another." We, the elders of _____, welcome evaluation by our peers. Knowing there are three primary criteria for serving in this capacity, we hold one another accountable in those very same areas of concern. After completing the following in writing, we dialog in conversation our responses with one another.

Category #1 CALLING
1) How, and to what degree, do you find personal satisfaction serving as an elder?
2) How has the Lord used you in this position of service?
3) To what degree do you look forward to continuing to serve as an elder?
4) How, and to what degree, do you sense a change in God's call on your life to serve as an elder?

Category #2 COMPETENCY
1) In what specific areas of ministry did you serve this past year?
2) How would you evaluate your service?
3) How would those within your sphere of influence evaluate your service?
4) How have ministry demands impacted your spiritual growth?
5) How, and to what degree, do you plan to develop specific competencies in your spiritual gifting?
6) What, if any, changes need to be made regarding your role as an elder? Will these changes enhance your competency?

7) Are there specific ways that we—or others—can enable you to serve more effectively as an elder? If so, please describe those suggestions.

Category #3 CHARACTER

1) Please describe your pursuit of spiritual disciplines (i.e., prayer, fasting, Bible reading, solitude, silence, etc.) in your life this past year.
2) How do you perceive sanctification is occurring in your life?
3) What intentional actions are you taking to protect your integrity?
4) Is there a brother in Christ holding you accountable with regard to your character? If not, why not? If so, how does that accountability relationship function?

Appendix 6.2

The following instrument is a compilation from similar instruments available on the market, and hence contains a "question bank" of possible items for an inventory.[5] This should *not* simply be copied and used in its present form. Rather, items should be carefully selected so as to tailor an instrument to your congregation. No one elder can fulfill *every expectation* on this list. Perhaps an elder may choose the top ten qualities that he does exhibit, and then assess his performance on those selected areas. The instrument could be completed by the individual elders and then by peers about that elder, so as to provide self-assessment balanced with peer assessment.

Assessment Item	Low High
I spend time with new members.	① ② ③ ④ ⑤
I call on congregation members.	① ② ③ ④ ⑤
I visit with members who are inactive.	① ② ③ ④ ⑤
I speak with members who are unhappy with our congregation.	① ② ③ ④ ⑤
I make evangelistic contacts.	① ② ③ ④ ⑤
I make calls on the sick or hospitalized.	① ② ③ ④ ⑤
I make contact with the congregation shut-ins.	① ② ③ ④ ⑤
I provide spiritual advice and counsel to individuals.	① ② ③ ④ ⑤
I encourage others in their Christian walk.	① ② ③ ④ ⑤
I greet people at church events, such as worship.	① ② ③ ④ ⑤
I teach a class or small group.	① ② ③ ④ ⑤
I give communion meditations in worship.	① ② ③ ④ ⑤
I lead the church in special projects.	① ② ③ ④ ⑤
I lead committees and taskforces.	① ② ③ ④ ⑤
I participate in regularly scheduled elder's meetings.	① ② ③ ④ ⑤
I am willing to assess church programs.	① ② ③ ④ ⑤
I provide feedback and evaluate the pastoral staff.	① ② ③ ④ ⑤

I am supportive of the pastoral staff.	① ② ③ ④ ⑤
I am involved at church in more than the worship service.	① ② ③ ④ ⑤
I give financially to the church.	① ② ③ ④ ⑤
I regularly pray for others.	① ② ③ ④ ⑤
I open my home to church activities and needs.	① ② ③ ④ ⑤
I openly support the vision of the church's ministry.	① ② ③ ④ ⑤
I have engaged in church discipline when necessary.	① ② ③ ④ ⑤
I make beneficial decisions for the congregation's best interest.	① ② ③ ④ ⑤
I feel I have grown spiritually in the past year.	① ② ③ ④ ⑤
I accurately communicate to the congregation's membership.	① ② ③ ④ ⑤

Identify *four* strengths that are evident in you as an elder:

①

②

③

④

Identify *one* area that need improvement in your service as an elder:

Endnotes

[1] Cf. James Estep, "Conducting Performance Reviews," *Management Essentials for Christian Ministries* (Nashville: Broadman and Holman, 2005), pp. 387-410.

[2] Michael Woodruff (1994), "Managing Your Ministry," *Youthworker* (Winter 1994), p. 38.

[3] Kenneth Gangel, *Team Leadership in Christian Ministry* (Chicago: Moody Press, 1997), p. 383.

[4] Jim Ryan, "Rewarding Good Performance," *Church Administration*, 40(1997), p. 28.

[5] Cf. Brett DeYoung, "One Church's Perspective on the Eldership," *Christian Standard* (March 24, 1991), pp. 250-251; Larry Kreider *et. al. The Biblical Role of Elders for Today's Church* (Ephrata, PN: House to House Publications, 2004), pp. 216-218.